MYSIA

◆Troy

TENEDOS

▲ Mount Ida

TURKEY

SCYROS

AEGEAN SEA

CRETE

DATELINE: TROY

✦

ALSO BY PAUL FLEISCHMAN

✦

Picture Books
Time Train
Shadow Play
The Birthday Tree
The Animal Hedge

Novels
A Fate Totally Worse Than Death
The Borning Room
Saturnalia
Rear-View Mirrors
Path of the Pale Horse
The Half-A-Moon Inn

Short Stories
Coming-and-Going Men: Four Tales
Graven Images: Three Stories

Poetry
I Am Phoenix: Poems for Two Voices
Joyful Noise: Poems for Two Voices

Nonfiction
Townsend's Warbler
Copier Creations

DATELINE: TROY

TROY

PAUL FLEISCHMAN

collages by
Gwen Frankfeldt &
Glenn Morrow

CANDLEWICK PRESS
CAMBRIDGE, MASSACHUSETTS

First edition 1996

Library of Congress Cataloging-in-Publication Data

Fleischman, Paul.
Dateline: Troy / Paul Fleischman ; collages by Gwen Frankfeldt & Glenn Morrow.—1st ed.
Summary: A retelling of the story of the Trojan War illustrated with collages featuring
newspaper clippings of modern events from World War I through the Persian Gulf war.
ISBN 1-56402-469-5
1. Trojan War—Juvenile literature. 2. Mythology, Greek—Juvenile literature.
3. World politics—20th century—Juvenile literature.
[1. Trojan War. 2. Mythology, Greek.] I. Frankfeldt, Gwen, ill.
II. Morrow, Glenn, ill. III. Title.
BL793.T7F57   1996
398.2'0938—dc20   95-36356

2 4 6 8 10 9 7 5 3 1

Printed in Hong Kong

This book was typeset in Centaur.
Book design by Virginia Evans

Candlewick Press
2067 Massachusetts Avenue
Cambridge, Massachusetts 02140

For

Nancy

&

Ethan Bronstein

◆

DATELINE: TROY

♦

THE NORTH WIND NOSES through the rubble that was Troy. Mighty Achilles has been dead for millennia. Ravishing Helen, old King Priam, truth-telling Cassandra—all have lain long in their graves, if indeed they actually lived.

The siege and sack of Troy is old news, more than three thousand years old. The story was ancient even to the ancient Greeks who sang it from memory. Yet sing it, then write it and read it, they did, as have innumerable tale-bearers since. The first book to be printed in English appeared in 1475 and recounted the Trojan War. In

1873 the site of Troy was discovered in western Turkey, facing Greece across the Aegean Sea. The city long thought mythical was real. Listeners and readers had always found real human nature in what had transpired there. Envy-maddened Ajax, lovestruck Paris, crafty Odysseus, and all the others have walked the earth in every age and place. They live among us today. Though their tale comes from the distant Bronze Age, it's as current as this morning's headlines. The Trojan War is still being fought. Simply open a newspaper....

It began with a nightmare.

Hecuba, queen of Troy, was with child. The night before the birth, she awoke shrieking. "The fire!" she cried out. "It spreads!"

King Priam bolted up. There was no fire. Hecuba had been dreaming. Shaking, she stammered what she'd dreamt: that instead of bearing a child, she'd brought forth a tangle of flaming snakes.

"Send for Calchas!" commanded Priam.

Old feet shuffled through the palace. Priest of Apollo, interpreter of omens, reader of dreams and the future, Calchas gave ear to the queen.

"The vision speaks plainly," he pronounced. "The child will bring fire and ruin upon Troy. There's but one course of action." He peered at the queen, then the king. "When it's born, cut the infant's throat."

MAY 1988

At first light Hecuba gave birth to a boy. She held him until noon, weeping all the while. Priam at last took the baby from her arms, but couldn't bring himself to kill him. Still, he knew what must be done. He had a herdsman brought to the palace and entrusted him with the child and the deed. "Take him high on Mount Ida," he instructed. "Seek an untraveled spot—and leave him." He touched his son's face, then the rattle his wife had pressed into his tiny hand. He turned away.

The herdsman obeyed and left the infant to die. Five days later he returned to the place—and gaped. No crow-pecked corpse lay before him, but a living baby, being suckled by a she-bear. Amazed, sure the boy was fated to live, the man carried him home to his wife.

The next day, he walked to Troy and presented Priam with a dog's tongue as proof that the prince was dead. He returned to his hut. He would raise the child in secret. He and his wife named him Paris.

12

✦

Salinas

Newborn Found In Dumpster

By Joe Livernois
Herald Salinas Bureau

SALINAS — A newborn infant found wrapped in a blood-stained pillowcase in a trash dumpster early Thursday morning was reported in good condition last night in a Salinas hospital.

The 6-pound boy was discovered in the trash bin outside a south Salinas apartment complex by a man who lives with the mother and who said he was not aware the woman was pregnant, Salinas police say.

The boy's mother, 26-year-old Audrey Garcia, of 60 Stephanie Drive, has been arrested on felony charges of child endangerment, according to Capt. Tom Brooks of the Salinas police.

She told officers that she put the child in the dumpster of the West Lake apartment complex after it was born because she did not want her boyfriend or her mother to find out about it, according to a police report.

Police Guard

Ms. Garcia was at Salinas Valley Memorial Hospital on Thursday for medical observation under police guard, Brooks said.

According to the police report, doctors at Salinas Valley Memorial reported the baby was suffering from hypothermia when he arrived at the hospital, but was in good health after treatment.

(AP Laserphoto, Copyright The Salinas Ca

NURSES CARE FOR NEWBORN BABY FOUND IN DUMPST
... Cindy Shea (left) and Ruthann Green delighted

Brooks said that Glen Douglas, 30, discovered the infant when he heard the baby crying from the dumpster as he walked through the apartment complex about 4:30 a.m. Thursday.

Douglas told police he first thought the baby's crying was "a cat meowing in anger."

When he looked in the du he found the baby in a yel lowcase spotted with blood.

Bath Towels

He took it to his apa wrapped it in bath towe called police.

JULY 1988

The lad grew up hardy, handsome, and as quick with his wits as his feet. He tended cattle, unaware that he was a prince. When the herdsmen set their bulls to fight, fair-minded Paris was often asked to judge the winner. Zeus, chief among all the gods, watching from his palace on Mount Olympus, took note of the young man.

It was at this time that the gods attended the wedding of the sea goddess Thetis. They'd all been invited, with one exception. Eris, the spiteful goddess of strife, had been shunned. Incensed, she plotted her retaliation, and in the midst of the festivities she flung a golden apple into the throng. Written upon it were the words: FOR THE FAIREST. Zeus' wife Hera assumed it was meant for her. Athena, goddess of wisdom and battle, boasted that her own beauty outshone Hera's. Appalled, Aphrodite, the goddess of love, insisted that the apple should be hers. Their quarrel grew vicious, halting the feast. Watching Eris grinned. Finally, Zeus had to be called on to choose the most comely of the three. He eyed them, knowing that the two he passed over would make his life a misery. He longed to pass the task to another.

It was then that he remembered Paris.

Studies on beauty raise a number of ugly findings

'Appearance is so important to our opinions of people, it's almost disgusting '

By Deborah Blum
McCLATCHY NEWS SERVICE

CHICAGO — In a sad little test of the importance of good looks, Pennsylvania scientists recently painted a large purple "birthmark" on the face of a woman and sent her out to ride an urban subway. At a stop for Philadelphia's Temple University's emergency medical center, she was instructed to throw herself down on the subway car floor in an apparent epileptic seizure.

"We wanted to see how long it would take before a Good Samaritan helped her across the street," said Albert Kligman, a professor of dermatology at the University of Pennsylvania. "Instead, the car just emptied out right over her. We tried it three different times and no one ever helped her."

Of course, when her face was mark-free, help came readily.

"It pays to be good-looking in this country," Kligman said during a session of the American Association of the Advancement of Science. "Appearance is so important to our opinions of other people, it's almost disgusting."

And baffling to scientists. In a recent gathering to explore the "Science of Beauty," they expressed their astonishment at how important attractiveness is in human relationships, apparently affecting even the bonds between mothers and infants.

I started doing research, that attrac-

said. "The good news is that no mother treated her baby unkindly. The bad news is the more attractive ones got a lot more attention."

But the reverse also may be true. Langlois has videotaped 3- and 6-month-old infants looking at pictures of pretty and plain women. Consistently, the infants turn away from the plain faces and stare longer at the pretty ones. At one point, the Texas scientists hired a very pretty woman to play with babies, but on alternate days she wore a mask, designed to recast her face into knobby features.

Why the babies smiled

Not only did babies look away from her when she wore the mask, they would actively try to move away from her. On the other hand, when she entered the room normally made up, the infants would stare at her and smile, and male babies, in particular, would move toward her.

She said that other studies have found similar results, although no one is sure how children so young would be able to assess attractiveness.

Allan Mazur, a sociologist at Syracuse University, pointed out that society's concepts of women's beauty have changed during the last century, particularly male judgment of what an attractive body should like like.

Mazur said that during the late 1800s, the standard requirement for chorus girls in New York City were decidedly sturdy: women about 5-feet-4 and 130 pounds.

"In the 1920s, a pear-shaped body was the ideal, with the hips being larger than the bust," Mazur said, citing movie actress Jean Harlow as a classic exa

He charted the bree
measurements given by Play
from the 1960s

"How can I choose without favor?" asked Zeus. "Hera is my wife, and Athena, my own daughter." He handed the apple to Hermes, the gods' messenger, and sent him winging away. "The Trojan herdsman Paris will judge instead. He's much admired for his impartial decisions. You'll find him on Mount Ida."

Grazing his cattle, Paris was agape when Hermes appeared and announced Zeus' will. He humbly tried to decline, but was refused. A moment later the goddesses alit.

They disrobed before a dumbstruck Paris. Nervously, he regarded Hera first. "Award me the apple," she coaxed, "and I'll make you emperor of all Asia." Athena, next, promised to make him the wisest of men and invincible in war. Then he came to Aphrodite. "I can make you emperor as well—of the heart, and invincible in love. Name the woman and she shall be yours."

Paris paused, distracted by this offer.

"Queen Helen of Sparta, for instance," Aphrodite continued. "The most beautiful woman in all the world, whose looks approach even my own."

Paris gazed upon the goddess' body, imagining she were Helen and his. Then he remembered. "But Helen is married."

"My magic will make her as a moth, and you a lantern. She'll follow you, entranced with passion, leaving her husband and home without a thought."

Paris' judgment buckled beneath the weight of this bribe. He took a step back. "I find Aphrodite the fairest," he announced, and placed the golden apple in her palm.

She nodded at him, sealing their pact, and gave her rivals a superior smile. Hera fumed. Athena's eyes blazed. Furious with Paris, the two stalked off, vowing revenge on him and all Trojans.

the queen

[...]ont Park, near where the queen's 412-foot [...]acht Britannia is docked.

That's where a black-tie dinner was held for [...] select group of guests, among them former [...]President Reagan and his wife Nancy, who [...]ore a long white gown, and former President [...]ord, and his wife, Betty, who wore a salmon-[...]olored chiffon gown.

The queen wore a form-fitting, floor-length [...]own and a dusty rose brocade with a diamond [...]ecklace and earrings.

As the guests boarded the yacht for dinner, [...] members loaded Florida citrus on the [...]t for the trip around the Keys.

[...] Booker T. Washington, students enter[...]d the queen with a 15-minute pageant on [...] city's history followed by a performance [...] the school's marching band. In addition [...]Rule Britannia," the band performed some [...] and rap scores, including the pop favorite [...]nna Make You Sweat."

[...]he queen, wearing a thin blue and white [...]k with a blue boater, smiled and clapped [...]litely. She did not seem bothered by the 88-[...]gree heat.

to Kuwait

[...]recog[...]-[...]inued [...]wait, [...] the [...]gov-[...]titute

passed Congress. The appropriations bill, now before a House-Senate conference committee, has a higher price tag because it also includes funds to reimburse the military for costs related to the relief effort.

The Pentagon said in its statement that the 11th Armored Cavalry Regiment, based in Fulda, Germany, will send elements of three squadrons to Kuwait in order to permit U.S. forces there to return to their home units.

[...]riday [...]o re-[...]r aid [...]thern

[...]on to [...]s bill [...]d the [...]not yet

The new troops are to be in place by mid-June and remain there until Sept. 1.

war veterans

[...] and [...]rit, a [...]tied [...] on

[...]icized [...]war, [...] for [...]d a [...]tion [...]uest [...]rned [...]troops

event is meant to be a homecoming for soldiers and not a glorification of war.

"I really don't have a concern, because the way this thing is laid out, we're just celebrating the welcome home, a job well done by the troops," said Grant, who is the city's honorary mayor of Hollywood and overseer of the Hollywood Walk of Fame.

The parade will feature a flyover by four stealth fighters, a B-25 bomber, a B-17 Flying Fortress, P-51 Mustangs and Condor AT-6s. Along the [...]

Associated Pre[...]

Miss Mexico was crowned Miss Universe last night in Las Vegas.

Mexico takes Miss Universe title; Miss U.S.A. in top six

LAS VEGAS (AP) — Lupita Jones, of Mexicali, Mexico, was crowned the new Miss Universe last night as hundreds of her countrymen cheered wildly at the televised pageant held on the glitzy Las Vegas strip.

[...]old beat out 20-.

Miss U.S.A., Kelli McCarty, 21, of Liberal, Kansas; Miss Venezuela, Jackeline Rodriguez, 19, and Miss Jamaica, Kimberly Mais, 21, rounded out the top six finalists.

Rounding out the top ten were [...] Vivian

The following day, his mind whirling with thoughts of Helen, Paris strode off toward Troy. An athletic competition was to be held there that afternoon. His foster father tried to dissuade him but ended up walking with him to the city. It was the first time Paris had set foot in Troy.

He began the competition by entering the boxing contest, and to the surprise of all, defeated Priam's sons. The proudhearted princes were unaccustomed to losing. Yet Paris flew past them in the footrace as well. At once they demanded a second race to be run. Paris left them behind again. Infuriated, they decided to kill him and drew their swords. Paris dashed for his life. His foster father threw himself before Priam. "Stop them, your Majesty!" he cried. "That youth is your own lost son!"

Priam recognized the old man, halted his sons, and rushed up to Paris. He stared into his face. Hecuba followed. The herdsman produced the silver rattle he'd found in the infant's hand years before. The king and queen knew it at once. Both burst out weeping, clutching Paris.

The old herdsman had feared he'd be punished. But that night, Priam invited him to a magnificent banquet to mark his son's return. When the seer Calchas heard the news, he and Apollo's other priests again warned the king to put Paris to death.

"Never!" replied Priam. "Better that Troy should burn than that my precious son should die!"

IN SEARCH OF DANIEL

A Mother Finds the Son She Gave Away

By **Laura Watkins Lewis**
Special to The Washington Post

On a fall morning more than half my life ago, I stood in front of the Florence Crittenton Home at the juncture of MacArthur Boulevard and Reservoir Road and watched a social worker drive away with my infant son. I was 17. I had been led to believe he would be happier if he were adopted and I were no longer part of his life. I was told I would get over the hurt and have other children to replace him. And I thought I would never see him again.

None of this was true, but I believed it.

In surrendering my child to adoption in the late 1960s, I was cast in an Orwellian drama that does not end. People should know what it is like to give up a child, or to be adopted. My son and I are experts. We have lived and breathed adoption. Perhaps I should say we survived it.

My son had to grow up with no factual or positive knowledge about me and his natural father. All he could know was that the parents who made him gave him into the unknown.

When I surrendered my baby, I had no idea what it could do to us. I knew nothing of the effects of secrecy in adoption or the subtle ways in which it affected me; I see these only in retrospect. I ripped out some pages from my journal over time because I could not bear to confront the pain and self-hatred. But most of it is intact.

For half my life, I anesthetized myself by parroting the rationalization that adoption was best for my child. It never dawned on me that I did not know if he were alive or dead, happy or sad, wanted or unwanted. A fantasy that he was in a perfect home with saint-like parents filled the void that was really there, keeping me together.

Because of my age, a legal abortion was offered during my third month by a reputable Washington gynecologist. Abortions were easy to get in 1967, if one's family had the money. I thought I would be allowed to keep my baby and left his office in tears. Six weeks later, a visibly pregnant 10th grader, I was expelled from my small private school. Gradually, the constant flow of messages from family and society that my pregnancy was a horrible mistake drove a wedge of fear into my relationship with my unborn child.

Then, in a burst of my parents' frustration, I was ordered to leave home. I found a room in a boarding house in exchange for helping with chores and got a job as a waitress under an assumed name. One day, three weeks later, I fainted and dropped a tray of pancakes and coffee on a customer. Because my parents had changed their minds and reported me as a runaway, detectives found me shortly afterward and brought me to a juvenile de-

See SEARCH, Page 15

more acceptable now for men to express an emotion-
says Robyn Quinter of the Adoptee-Birthparent
Network. "And men today, especially those 20 to
... re sensitive to their needs since they're more
... uldbirth and child-rearing."
... decision to search is tied to a significant
... rcher's life, such as marriage, the birth of
... e searcher her first link to a blood rel-
... th of an adopted family member. Some
... they were left for adoption, while oth-
... "feel a need to tell the birthparents
... right decision."
... ite medical reasons, such as a need to
... ry diseases, allergies, visual disorders
... hey may be susceptible to. But the mo-
... entioned is a need to be connected with

... like? Who are you? I don't think there's
adopted person was disconnected from
Roberta Ross of Adoptees in Search

See ADOPTION, Page 15

Paris exchanged his dirt-floored hut for a room of polished stone in the palace. Soon afterward, Menelaus, king of Sparta, chanced to visit Troy. Knowing that he was Helen's husband, Paris prodded him, heart pounding, to describe his bewitching wife. He so shrewdly cultivated the king's friendship that Menelaus invited the prince to accompany him home and be his guest in turn. Feverish with joy, Paris accepted.

Aphrodite sent their ship fair winds. They reached Sparta and marched up toward the palace. A woman stood in wait. Paris approached, then halted in awe. Flesh bested fancy. She had the grace of a deer and a dewdrop's radiance. He feared that such an earthly wonder would take no notice of a cowherd-prince. Had Aphrodite cast her promised spell? He watched as the queen embraced her husband. The goddess, however, had been true to her word. Helen set her eyes upon Paris and fell instantly, irresistibly in love.

For nine days Paris feasted with his hosts. He yearned to shout out his love for Helen and wrote her name in wine spilled on the table. Menelaus, cast down by the news that his father had just died in Crete, took no notice. On the tenth morning, he departed for the funeral.

The lovers exulted at their good fortune. Paris had first imagined Helen, then beheld. At last he'd be able to touch her. Love-maddened, the two decided to leave Sparta that night and never return.

Attract the opposite sex — with secret signals

The way you smile, speak or even stand can help you attract the opposite sex, reveals an expert. Dr. David Givens, author of the book *Love Signals*, spent four years studying American meeting rituals — and here he offers some of the secret sig-

nals men and women can use to attract the opposite sex:

RAISED SHOULDERS — This gives a signal of harmlessness. Marilyn Monroe used

this gesture, and right now Jessica Lange has the most seductive shoulders of all.

THE COY LOOK — "Gaze down, as if you're looking at your feet, then lift your eyes and look at the person's face," said Dr. Givens. "It's submissive, but it invites contact."

TOES POINTED IN — "If you stand pigeon-toed, it gives the other person permission to come closer because they know that you're interested. It's another sign of submissiveness."

FORWARD LEAN — "If you're seated across from someone, a good way to convey interest without being too bold is to swivel your upper body so that it's facing the person, then lean toward them just a little without even looking at them.

"The gesture doesn't have to be exaggerated — remember that courtship works best with a subtle cue, not a full stampede forward."

OPEN SMILE — "Part your lips and show your upper teeth. It's a more direct sign of liking than a closed smile."

SOFT VOICE — "Use the same voice you would with children or pets. A slightly lower

volume gives message you'

HALF-CL "This is a ward the er ter touchi It's an in

ACTIV "Tip you and rai person never

"A mou son te

In darkness the pair carried the palace treasures aboard their ship and set off. They headed for Troy, but Hera, pouncing on the chance to punish Paris for denying her the golden apple, raised a great storm that blew them far off course. Landing at Cyprus, they stayed several months, fearing Menelaus lay in wait off Troy. They then sailed to the city of Sidon, whose king Paris murdered and whose coffers he emptied, adding vast stores of gold to their hold.

At last they reached Troy, welcomed by cheers and celebrations. The Trojans were dazzled not only by the riches but by Helen, more exquisite than any gem. Entranced, they swore never to see her returned. Hadn't the Greeks refused to send back Priam's own sister, carried away from Troy by a band of Greeks years before? As for the priests who'd joined Calchas in urging that Paris be killed, Paris silenced them with generous gifts of gold to Apollo's temple.

Only one voice was raised against Paris. It came from his own sister, Cassandra, a prophetess who'd been doomed by the god Apollo never to be believed. Over and over she'd warned Priam not to let Paris travel to Sparta. Now she declared that a frightful war would result unless Helen were sent back at once. The king listened patiently to his daughter. Then, as he had many times before, he sent her away, ignoring her words.

WORLD NE

CRISIS IN THE GULF

Some Iraqis Call Occupation of Kuwait Immoral

By Tod Robberson
Washington Post Foreign Service

BAGHDAD, Iraq

While President Saddam Hussein prepares his nation for war, ordinary citizens such as housewives, students, businessmen and taxi drivers are debating the righteousness of Saddam's crusade against Kuwait—and some say that what he has done to the tiny Persian Gulf emirate is immoral.

Although Iraqis seem to have a deeply ingrained resentment of Kuwaitis and their flaunting of oil wealth, many—both Moslems and Christians—have vowed, for example, not to purchase any product that they believe has been stolen from Kuwait.

"If I know something was purchased legitimately, I buy it," said an Iraqi businessman. "But if I think it was stolen, I don't."

Another persistent topic of conversation here is about the prospect of war and Iraq's resolve to fight after having just emerged from a debilitating eight-year war with Iran. Some have vowed to fight to the death. Others are bone-weary of conflict.

One woman said that in the year and a half since the Iran-Iraq war ended, "people were just starting to relax. There was a big sigh of relief. And then this started. Nobody wants to go to war again. We are all so tired of it."

To be sure, Iraqis more often than not will tell reporters what the government wants them to say, rather than what they really feel.

Before the television cameras and tape recorders of the international media, Iraqis will say that their fealty to Saddam is unwavering, that their support for his occupation of Kuwait is rock-solid, that their willingness to die for their country—on the battlefield in Kuwait or by U.S. bombs in Baghdad—is unquestionable.

But in the privacy of their own homes, the story is often quite different. Below the surface of public spectacle in this country is a mood of uncertainty, fear, doubt and even outrage over the Iraqi occupation of Kuwait and the potential it has raised for war against a U.S.-led multinational force. Intermixed with these

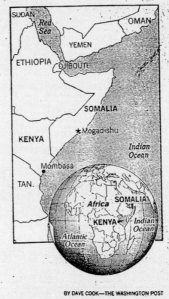

BY DAVE COOK—THE WASHINGTON POST

Evacuees Tell
Bodies Said to Litter Ca

By Neil Henry
Washington Post Foreign Service

MOMBASA, Kenya, Jan. 6—Of all t horrors 45-year-old Mohamud Aden Yus encountered during 10 days he spent cently in Mogadishu, the war-ravaged c ital of Somalia, he said none surpassed grisly sight of 35 dead Somali soldiers ing in a perfectly straight row on a dov town street, rotting in the afternoon su

"Why don't you bury these peop! Yusuf said he asked several young reb guarding their human trophies close weapons in hand. "Why do you leave th like this to waste away?"

Because President Mohamed S Barre's men did the same thing to a re squad last year, one of the youths repli "This is eye for eye," he told Yus:f.

Following his father's funeral, Menelaus had sailed home from Crete. No Helen waited to welcome him. His trusted guest was gone as well. In a fury he stormed through the looted palace, astounded at Paris' treachery. Then he remembered the oath.

Years back, when Helen had reached marriageable age, a flock of suitors had descended on Sparta. Many were kings and princes. All were drunk with desire, so dangerously so that her father had feared that the one he chose would be murdered by the others. To keep their swords sheathed, he'd proposed an oath: each suitor would swear to defend Helen's husband against any man who tried to steal her away. Since all had hoped to gain this protection, each of them had taken the oath. He'd then given Helen to the wealthiest of her wooers, Menelaus.

Enraged to picture her now with Paris, Menelaus sped north to the city of Mycenae. He burst forth with the news to his brother Agamemnon, the High King, most powerful of all the Greek rulers, and reminded him of the suitors' pledge. Agamemnon, married to Helen's sister, listened to the tale in shock. At once he sent heralds to all the former suitors, calling them to make good their oaths. Each would contribute soldiers or ships, making up a vast army and fleet. Though its walls were towering and thick, Troy would be taken, he vowed, and Helen with it.

ARMY CALL GOING TO 896 RESERVISTS

Two-Thirds of State's Quota Are Combat Officers Facing Tests Aug. 23, Duty Sept. 22

Mandatory calls to active duty will go out to 896 Army Reserve officers—two-thirds of them combat lieutenants and captains—in New York State within a few weeks.

Col. H. A. Cooney, chief of the New York Military District, announced yesterday the state's quota in the first involuntary call-up of ground force reservists not attached to Organized Reserve units.

First orders will be issued next week summoning men to report for physical examinations at Army installations near their homes Aug. 23. Thereafter, the first of those accepted will be ordered to active duty by Sept. 22.

New York's quota of reservists includes 197 captains and 651 lieutenants from combat and service arms; two majors and thirty-nine captains or lieutenants from the Medical Service Corps and two majors, four captains and one lieutenant from the Veterinary Corps. Colonel Cooney said he expected further calls for medical and dental officers.

Men will be selected from both the volunteer reserve—those nominally assigned to a volunteer unit but not active in it—and from the inactive reserve—former officers who have taken no part in reserve activities since their separation from active duty.

Officers assigned to Organized Reserve units generally will not be called to active duty before their unit as a whole is called up.

Tightening of Deferments

Younger officers would be selected first, a spokesman said, but calls might be issued to any reservists within the "age-in-grade" limits if necessary to fill quotas. For the combat arms, maximum ages are 30 years for second lieutenants, 35 for first lieutenants and 41 for captains. For the noncombat services the comparable age limits are 38, 41 and 45.

Individuals or employers seeking deferment of reservists would required to take steps upon r to report for physical exam

A spokesman warned

MARINES COVER

Mach

ALLIES BATTLING TO REGAIN POHANG

Continued From Page 1

was around the vital United States advanced airbase near Pohang, where North Korean regulars and guerrillas launched a drive to start again the left hand prong of their planned double envelopment down both coasts of the peninsula.

Last night United States —with cooks, clerks and ground crews in the line— tight a perimeter around field, which a tank and column had punched th their relief.

Communications H

This morning th was being held communica road th base left

G. I.
As
Hed

AUGUST 1950

Most of the suitors were quick to join the cause. King Diomedes of Argos, King Idomeneus of Crete, mighty Ajax, Prince Palamedes—all agreed to fight for Menelaus. Others were less enthusiastic.

Odysseus, king of Ithaca, schemed to escape his oath altogether. Palamedes, sent to recruit Odysseus, found him feigning insanity, plowing the sand at the shore with an ox and donkey and sowing salt in the furrows. Knowing the king's reputation for cunning, Palamedes set Odysseus' infant son directly before the ox's hooves. At once Odysseus reigned in his team, disproving his madness and revealing his ruse. He gave himself up to Palamedes and loaded his ships with soldiers.

While they journeyed from Ithaca, the Trojan priest Calchas traveled to Greece to consult an oracle, who instructed him to join the Greek forces. He did so, foretelling that they'd never take Troy unless they enlisted a prince named Achilles. This prince was the son of the sea goddess Thetis, whose wedding had been ruined by the golden apple. As her husband was human, not an immortal god, she'd sought to defend the child against death by dipping him into the protecting waters of the river Styx, forgetting that the heel she'd held him by had remained dry. Being partly divine, Achilles had grown to manhood in a matter of months.

Terrified at learning her son was needed by the Greeks, Thetis sent him to hide on the island of Scyros. There Achilles lived in the palace, disguised as a woman at his mother's insistence. And there Odysseus, sent by Agamemnon, finally found him. Disguised as well, as a peddler, Odysseus opened his trunk and displayed his wares. The palace women fingered his jewelry and fabrics. One, however, reached at once for the bronze sword he'd included. Odysseus grabbed him and tugged off his dress. The following day, eager for battle, Achilles sailed off to war.

Troops Ordered to Baltics to Capture Draft Dodgers

■ Soviet Union: Four other restive republics are targeted in a Kremlin effort to enforce national law.

By JOHN-THOR DAHLBURG
TIMES STAFF WRITER

MOSCOW—The Soviet Defense Monday ordered army reportedly by the ...own and cap-...ers in

...tion, held in the autumn, tumbled as alarmingly low as 10% of the draftable 18-year-olds in the re-public of Georgia, according to official sources.

The crackdown on draft dodging was the latest in a series of Gorba-chev's actions that show the grow-ing clout of traditionally conserva-tive institutions such as the armed ...es, the KGB and the Interior ...in forcing a toughe-...e on law and or-...security affairs. ...applies ...

Draft Evaders Taking Canadian Citizenship

...sbaud U.S. Ai... ...and Mrs. Rich-

...tary Wife of the Year... She and her husband live in Sacramento.

New York Times News Service

MONTREAL — Stanley J. Elizabeth," does not Pietlock, a 39-year-old draft constitute renunciation ...or from Wilmington, Del., ...can citizenship, but it ...y became a citizen of practically the same taking an irrevocable ...ing the United Sta-is being chosen by ...ment grounds to re-the young antiwar ...citizenship, whenev-...re ...that he has becon-...big ...hing, and sure it ...Although these ...ional" recalled Piet- are still just as ...who now teaches ever were to ...in Toronto. "But the ...ward Canadi-...ole thrust of my life has be- the United St-...come Canadian, so it made a new dime-...ence ... over wheth-

Pietlock is in the first ranks granted a ... of what is expected to become a Almost ... wave of newly-naturalized Cana- exiles an ... dians who left the United States cause th-... to avoid serving in Vietnam. ...unconce-...it was five years ago, in the us of a ... that the trick-...

780 White South Africans Vow to Resist Draft

By CHRISTOPHER S. WREN
Special to The New York Times

JOHANNESBURG, Sept. 21 — In the largest concerted campaign so far to resist conscription, more than 780 whites of military age pledged today to refuse to serve in South Africa's armed forces

The announcement was made at simultaneous news conferences in six South African cities. Those coming for-ward identified themselves as not only young men awaiting conscription but also as reservists, including 49 com-missioned and noncommissioned offi-cers, who said they would r...annual call-up.

South Africa requires all white males to serve two years in its armed forces, followed by annual reserve training. The country's black majority is not subject to the draft

There is a provision for alternative service in civilian institutions by con-scientious objectors, but only on reli-gious grounds. Refusal ...armed forces is pu...years in prison and ...among them ...Beseter and ...jail for ...

ages conscientious objection. ...been effectively banned unde-...tionwide state-of-eme-...though the group ann-...that it planned to r-...A spokesm-

...1991

Thousands of mothers protest Yugoslavia army conscription

BY TONY SMITH
Associated Press

OSIJEK, Yugoslavia — About 10,000 mothers chanting "Serb army get out!" swarmed around a federal army building yesterday demanding the re-lease of their conscript sons.

The march was part of a nationwide protest of the killing in Yugoslavia. Women also held rallies in Belgrade, the federal capital, and in Croatia's capital, Zagreb.

A few hundred mothers carrying Croatia's checker-board flag and banners reading "Down with the gen-erals!" marched through downtown Osijek before joining thousands more outside the army cultural and recreation center.

They demanded the release of their sons from the Yugoslav People's Army. The federal military has be-come increasingly involved in clashes between Croatian forces and armed Serb rebels in the scarred Croatian region of Slavonia, bord...

Croatia accuses the army, with its ...officer corps, of backing the Serb r-...erals say their tanks are out to ...parties.

More than 50 busloads of mothers from Croa... and the republics of Macedonia and Bosn... Hercegovina traveled to Belgrade to petition a... generals to release their sons from service.

Initially Bosnia and Macedonia were neutral i... conflict between Croatia and Serbia, but increa... they have leaned toward Croatia.

In Osijek, protesting mothers converged ... army center and shouted at the soldiers ... "Come out, come out, you cowards!"

"Serb army get out! March back to Serbia!" ...

Some mothers wept. Others clutched re... and-blue flags and placards comparing th... Yugoslav acronym, JNA, to the Nazi swas... death's head symbols.

A small group, led by a gray-haired gra... lighted candles and then approached the... crowned by the once ubiquitous Commu... ...and Unity."

...ide the entrance hal... ...and retreated u...

...shouted ...afe in ta...

Mother talks with Federal Yugoslav Army commander in Belgrade.

Associated Press

...EC envoy accuses federal arm...

STOP THE EUROMISSILES

MAY 1973–AUGUST 1991

...what ...s be ...ster ...stiani ...ept 16 ...ay ...d

...ollide

...Air ...lumn ...sh village ...ople.

...nt Jaguar ...he collided ...160 ...and

Henry Wijnaendts, (who... Vukovar on Wednesday, dis... ...that.

...script in the Yugoslav... ...brade to de... ...tight attmamen...

A thousand ships, from every corner of Greece, gathered at Aulis for the invasion. Though Agamemnon promised his soldiers success, he knew that Troy would not be easily taken. Solemnly, he sacrificed one hundred fine bulls to almighty Zeus, beseeching him to favor the Greeks. From one hundred fires the scent of roasting meat, beloved by the gods, rose toward the heavens. The following morning the fleet set sail.

WAR IN THE GULF

legation to Iran

r nations to discuss end to war

hran report said.
delegation was head-
Prime Minister Sa-
adi, a member of
Revolutionary Com-
il, a tight, eight-man
President Saddam
madi was carrying a
Saddam to President
afsanjani, the report
parently traveled out
and, crossing the bor-
Iranian province of
ortheast of Baghdad.
the heels of the first
clash of the war and
rsial flight to Iran of

Iraqi planes, including sophisticated bombers and fighters, the Tehran talks will take place in the
shadow of an expanding conflict.

Some political analysts have
suggested the time might also be
ripe for Saddam to cut his losses,
declare his confrontation with the
American-led forces a victory and
withdraw from Kuwait before allied bombing wrecks his own military machine. But others doubt
that the Iraqi president would consider withdrawal before his ground
forces engage the coalition armies,
if then.

r cultivates pen pals

f them acquired
Sailor" mail sent
e United States.
sconsin, wrote
didn't want
ilors. "She
ber and
ing hap-
ourse
ed.

After allied planes started
bombing Iraqi targets, Stallins
said he asked his family to call
Heather and tell her he was OK.

Stallins said he also appreciates
the effort made by Cory, a 6-year-
old boy from New Jersey. "He
doesn't write much, because he's
only 6, but he does take the time to
write."

Associated Press

PRAYER BREAKFAST: Bush bows head
as George Gallup offers a prayer.

Bush declares this Sunday to be day of prayer

By the Los Angeles Times

WASHINGTON — President Bush has declared
Sunday a national day of prayer.

"I encourage all people of faith to say a special
prayer on that day — a prayer for peace; a prayer
for the safety of our troops; a prayer for their
families; a prayer for the innocents caught up in
this war," Bush said in a speech to the annual National Prayer Breakfast.

Also yesterday, Bush told visitors in a private
meeting that he will not authorize a Persian Gulf
cease-fire to give Saddam Hussein another chance
to withdraw his forces from Kuwait, but he also
has no plans to send U.S. ground troops on th
offensive anytime soon.

According to representatives of American
ish organizations, who spent an hour with
after returning from a five-day trip to Isr
president described Hussein as "an ev
whose aggressive behavior must be sto

With the war now in its third wee
peared to be devoting much of his tir
and public efforts to maintain supp
effort, as reports of the first U
ground combat reached comm
country.

AM-9 PM*! OPEN EARLY SATURDAY AT 9 AM

SUPER SAL

NAME FASHIONS FOR HI

At once Aphrodite rushed to Troy's aid by raising a gale that carried the ships far to the south toward Mysia. Upon landing, the Greeks battled the Mysians and lost hundreds of men before fleeing in their ships. Again Aphrodite stirred up a storm, scattering the fleet like leaves. Scores of ships sank. Leaking and lost, the rest struggled to return to Aulis. Though they'd yet to cast their eyes on Troy, a full third of the Greeks had perished.

Dead patients are removed from Athalassa Psychiatric Hospital in Nicosia as a wound-

ed patient awaits aid after Turkish air-craft bombed the hospital on Saturday.

Associated ...

The yard of the Athalassa psy-

reports that thr.....Greek ships were sunk. Greece denied the Turkish claim.

Ambassador-at-large Rob-ert J. McCloskey said the governments of Greece and Turkey would confirm the cease-fire at 3 a.m. EDT, or 9 a.m. Athens-time and 10 a.m. Ankara time.

The U.S. government an-nounces that the govern-ments of Greece and Turkey agree to the cease-fire as provided in the Security Council resolution of July 20, 1974, at 1400 GMT (10 a.m. EDT) on July 22," Mc-Closkey said shortly after midnight.

Department spokesmen said the U.S. proposal went to the governments in Athens and Ankara at 6 p.m. EDT yesterday after intense diplomatic contacts. It followed an intensive round of shuttle diplomacy between the two capitals by Undersecretary of State Joseph Sisco.

Sisco was reported to have said last night that "time is running out" for reaching an agreement as both NATO countries con-tinued to mobilize.

The fighting on Cyprus began last Monday between the 10,000-man Cypriot Na-tional Guard, led by Greek officers, and supporters for the Cypriot President, Arch-bishop Makarios, who was overthrown in a coup by the National Guard.

Conflict on the island spread to include battles be-tween the National Guard and the Turkish Cypriot community and Turkish troops which landed on Cy-prus on Saturday. The in-vasion of the island by Tur-key raised fears of a broader conflict among NATO allies.

Pressure Buil

White House Invita

By Lou Cannon
Washington Post Staff Writer

When Rep. William S. Co-hen of Maine was invited for a cruise aboard the presidential yacht Sequoia that subsequently was can-celed, fellow Republican Tom Railsback of Illinois said it was just as well.

"It probably would have been the first time" cracked Railsback, "that they would have taken the Sequoia into shark-infested waters."

Railsback's quip reflects the growing recognition among Republican members of the House Judiciary Com-mittee of the mounting po-litical pressure faced by GOP congressmen who are contemplating voting for the impeachment of President Nixon.

"The White House has taken a count and they know they've lost the com-mittee," said one Republican member last week. "Their only hope is to keep the vote down and try to pull it out in the House."

Few Republicans now ap-pear to believe that Nixon can avoid an impeach-ment trial in the Senate.

Second ranking commit-tee Republican Robert McC-of Illinois was merely say-out loud what his....

would m.....
vote for N....

McClo....
that he....
would....
cept th....
menda....

As t.....
move.....
floor....
findi....
ever....
from....
ann.....
wil....

R.....
P.....
c....

Greek Landing on Cyprus Repulsed, Turkey Reports

By John Saar
Washington Post Staff Writer

ANKARA, July 22 (Mon-day) — Turkish naval and air forces intercepted a Greek flotilla trying to land forces on Cyprus and inflict-ed "heavy losses," the Turk-ish General Staff announced last night.

The announcement said that the Greek landing operation was turned back "after repeated assaults" on Paphos in southwest Cyp-rus. Some of the Greek ships were sunk, the Turks said.

[In Athens, the Greek government called the claims "completely un....." and said it had

been "fabricated for domes-tic consumption and to mis-lead world public opinion."]

Early this morning, the British Broadcasting Co. monitored here, quoted re-ports from southwestern Turkey that "many Greek aircraft have landed on Rhodes, a Greek island, 12 miles off the coast of Tur-key and 240 miles west of Cyprus.

The report said the air-craft included combat and transport planes carry-ing troops.

The report led to specula-tion that Greece may be planning a military maneu-ver to counteract the Turk-ish invasion of Cyprus Satur-day—the Turkish response to

last Monday's coup in which a Greek-officered force over-threw Cypriot President Archbishop Makarios.

[However, Greece later said that it accepts "in toto" a U.N. resolution call-ing for a cease-fire on the island, in conjunction with a Security Council meeting.]

The sharp increase in mil-itary activity came as U.S. Under Secretary of State Jo-seph J. Sisco continued his shuttle diplomacy, arriving in Athens from Ankara. He was reported to have said in Athens last night after con-ferring with Greek leaders that "time is running out."

Athens Radio quoted him

See TURKEY, A10, Col. I

Department....
the propos....
by both....
las....

JULY 1974

Agamemnon readied his men to sail again. Yet day upon day a ferocious north wind blew. Knowing his ships would be driven far south, he waited for the wind to change. Weeks passed. Provisions and patience ran low. At last Agamemnon asked Calchas the cause.

"The goddess Artemis," answered the seer. "When you last killed a stag, you boasted that even she, goddess of the hunt, could not have made a better shot with her bow. The wind won't change until you've humbled yourself with a sacrifice to her, and a dread one at that—your daughter Iphigenia."

"Never!" roared the king, and sent Calchas from his sight.

The evil wind held. The muttering among the Greek leaders grew almost as loud. Agamemnon felt pinned. He cherished his beautiful daughter but longed to capture Troy and gild his name with glory. Then he overheard plans to replace him with a man of more mettle, such as Palamedes. At once Agamemnon made his choice. He sent for Iphigenia.

She arrived in Aulis, having been told that her father wished her to wed Achilles. Agamemnon, weighted with shame, then revealed the truth. Angered that his name had been used to lure Iphigenia to her doom, Achilles now strove to save her. Iphigenia, though, made no protest. "My life's but a little thing," she spoke. "Willingly will I give it up for the sake of so noble a cause."

Agamemnon viewed her through tears as she walked to the altar and placed her head on the stone. The priest's heavy knife hung in the air like a hawk. Then it dove at her neck.

That night, the wind slackened, then shifted to the west. At sunrise the Greeks set a course for Troy.

War Protester Burns Herself to Death Here

Immolation of Viet Peace Advocate Takes Place in Front of Federal Building

A woman who left a purse and a pickup truck filled with literature and other references to the anti-Vietnam war movement burned herself to death with gasoline Sunday on the steps of the Federal Building here.

Police identified her as Mrs. Florence Beaumont, 56, of 640 Sandia Ave., La Puente, wife of a commercial artist and mother of daughters 18 and 20.

Her husband, George, said later that she had "a deep feeling against the slaughter in Vietnam" and "must have felt she had to do this."

He said his wife had often told him, "It's not worth living when you have no redress from your representatives. All you receive from them is form letters."

The immolation took place at 1:07 p.m. in front of the building at 300 N. Los Angeles St. A federal guard tried to douse the flames which enveloped the woman with a fire extinguisher but was too late.

Partially Filled Gasoline Can

Police said Mrs. Beaumont apparently died before the flames were put out.

Her purse, found beside the point at which she ignited herself with a book of matches, contained several identity cards but no suicide note, police said.

Near the purse on a low wall in front of the building was a partially filled 2-gallon can of gasoline.

Witnesses said the woman ran about 40 feet, flaming and screaming, before she collapsed.

On the outside of the purse was a taped card reading, "Hello, I'm Florence Beaumont."

Inside was a voter's registration slip dated Sept. 26, 1967, at which time Mrs. Beaumont apparently registered to vote under the Peace and Freedom Party, a third party which has been formed to pursue an antiwar drive.

In a pickup truck the woman had parked nearby was literature advertising appearances by antiwar fi-

Over smooth seas the fleet sailed to the island of Tenedos, within sight of Troy. The Greeks were ravenous for battle. But Agamemnon could think only of Iphigenia and the men already lost. Before spilling more blood, he sent Menelaus and Odysseus to Troy to demand the return of Helen and the Spartan treasure.

The envoys addressed King Priam and his council. If their appeal was refused, they warned, the Greeks would destroy Troy. The great hall rang with bold defiance. "Let the Greeks come!" bellowed the Trojans. Never, they swore, would Helen be taken. Only one man, Antenor, declared that the Greek demands were just. At once he was shouted into silence and denounced as disloyal to Troy. Angry voices called for Menelaus and Odysseus to be killed. Scorned and jeered, it was only with Antenor's aid that they escaped that night with their lives.

Thwarted are the peacemakers

FROM OUR SPECIAL CORRESPONDENT IN CENTRAL AMERICA

THE momentum is gone from the plan, launched by President Oscar Arias of Costa Rica last August, by which Central Americans were going to work out their own peace. Once more, the region's most important diplomacy is being done in Washington. At the close of their meeting in Costa Rica on January 16th, Mr Arias's discordant club of five presidents from the region announced that it was setting no new deadline for compliance with the agreement. It was deadlines that distinguished the Arias plan from the long-winded and ineffectual Contadora peace talks that preceded it. The region's leaders have slipped back to open-ended promises.

The Arias plan had brie...

will not give effect to the amnesty for about 1,500 political prisoners which he drew up in November (though he is willing to release them if another country will take them in). Some of his supporters, and all his opponents, say that continuation of the war would spell darker things than that. They reckon Mr Ortega would reimpose the state of emergency and slam the lid back on the limited press freedom he has allowed in recent months.

Mr Ortega has made two conce... on the form of the ceasefire talks, bu... on the substance. He has agree... should be held in Central A... Costa Rican capital...

Ending months of indecision, Premier Mussolini, dictator of Fascist Italy, today announced declaration of war upon France and Great Britain. He thus leads his nation into war on the side of Germany. The dictator is pictured in characteristic uniform of a corporal in the blackshirts.

SENATORS HANGED IN EFFIGY.

[BY A. P. NIGHT WIRE.]

SAN ANSELMO (Cal.) April 5.— The six United States Senators who voted yesterday against the war resolution were hanged in effigy here tonight by former residents of Missouri, Wisconsin and Oregon. After being pronounced dead, the dummies were cut down and burned while the crowd sang "America."

Arafat Vows to 'Chop Off Hands' of 3 Peacemakers

From Times Wire Services

Much of the Arab world seethed with hatred and sorrow Monday, the day of peace for Egypt and Israel. Palestinian leader Yasser Arafat vowed to "chop off the hands" of "the stooge Sadat, the terrorist Begin and the imperialist Carter."

"This is my worst day since I left my home in Palestine in 1948," a Palestinian tailor, Mohammed Khaldi, told a reporter in Beirut. "I wish I were dead rather than be alive and witness this stigma and disgrace."

Effigies of President Carter, Israeli Prime Minister Menachem Begin and Egyptian President Anwar Sadat went up in flames in Palestinian refugee camps in Beirut and elsewhere in...

...ington and injured a number of people. In Tehran, Iran, protesters seize... the Egyptian Embassy and four em... ployes as hostages but said th... would not be harmed.

A mob stormed the Egyptian E... bassy in the Persian Gulf oil stat... Kuwait, smashing doors and windo... Protesters occupied the office... Egypt Air in Damascus, Syria.

In other world capitals, Pale... ans, other Arabs and sympa... paraded, staged sit-ins and ral... denounce the signing of a trea... ends 30 years of war between... and Egypt but leaves Israel in... of some occupied Arab lands a... not meet Arab demands for... pendent Palestinian homela...

Duce's War Speech Is Wildly Cheered

Months of Hesitation End as Mussolini Tells Of War Declaration

ROME, June 10. (AP) Via Radio —Italy tonight took the plunge into war at the side of Germany.

Premier Mussolini made the announcement in a bombastic speech from the balcony of the Palazzo Venezia before a wildly cheering crowd of fascists.

Italy's declaration of war, Mussolini said, had been handed to the ambassadors of France and England.

The fateful step was made after weeks—even months—of hesitation to weld into actual hostilities the ends of the long existent axis between Berlin and Rome.

Argentine President: Ready for Costly War

By Jackson Diehl
Washington Post Foreign Service

BUENOS AIRES, May 1—Argentine President Leopoldo Galtieri declared in a defiant midnight television address to the nation that Argentina was prepared to fight a costly war with Britain over the Falkland Islands.

Responding to Britain's attacks on the F... Army commander-in-chief said that Argen... ...doned its willingness to seek peace throu... "Argentina has responded with fire... ...be our response if the... ...into a...

APRIL 1917–JANUARY 1988

The Greeks seethed over the envoys' treatment. Bronze helmets polished, shields inspected, spear tips glittering like stars, they sailed across the strait the next day and saw Trojans by the thousands charging toward the beach. A hail of arrows kept the ships from landing. Achilles prepared to leap ashore but was held back by Calchas. "Let another!" cried the priest. "The first to land will be the first slain." This prophecy paralyzed the Greeks. At last a soldier named Protesilaus sprang from his ship and plunged into battle. With his comrades rushing ashore behind him, he struck down Trojans, then challenged King Priam's son Hector. At once he was speared through the throat.

At dusk the armies parted, taking their dead. That night, across the Aegean Sea, Protesilaus' wife learned in a dream that her husband had been killed. They'd just been wed. When he'd left to fight, she'd missed him so desperately that she'd had a statue made of him and often embraced it. Awaking now, raving with grief, she prayed to Persephone, goddess of death, who out of pity released her husband to visit her for the space of three hours. The two spoke and wept. When the time expired, he set off to return to the kingdom of the dead. Frantic at being parted from him forever, his wife seized a knife and stabbed herself. The two spirits journeyed to the underworld together.

This photograph of a grieving widow in a Denver cemetery on Memorial Day 1984 won a Pulitzer Prize for photographer Anthony Suau.

The glory and the waste

On the soil of 39 states and 12 foreign lands are spread silent tents by the tens of thousands, the eternal bivouac of America's war dead. Now taps sound again for 141 more, the epitaph of Desert Storm. Here's a Memorial Day memoir on the horror of it all.

BY SAUL PETT
Associated Press

Memorial Day, 1991. The United States has now fought 11 wars, the latest being the least, if not the last. In all, from Concord to Kuwait, 38,290,000 Americans have gone to war and 1,153,541 have not come back.

Their graves stretch across the country and around the world. More than 100,000 other Americans, probably many more,

foreign foe. Then come the Germans, Japanese, Vietnamese, Koreans, Mexicans, Spaniards, British, Indians (American) and Iraqis.

Now taps sound again at Arlington National Cemetery, this time for the dead home from the Persian Gulf. The first is an investment counselor from Grand Rapids, Mich., who joins George Washington's Continental soldiers in America's most distinguished cemetery.

Capt. Jonathan Edwards, a Marine pilot and reservist, volunteered for active duty in December, landed in Saudi Arabia in January, died in February in the crash of his helicopter and was buried here two weeks later.

Six white Shropshire horses pulled the caisson carrying the urn of his ashes, the mournful clip-clop joined with a slow drumroll. A three-volley farewell by an honor guard. Taps. And the flag held over

The Greeks pulled their ships far up onto the beach and built their camp before them. The following dawn they marched toward Troy, shaking spears and shouting taunts—but found no opponent coming forth to meet them. The men stared up at the reason: Troy's walls. Built of massive blocks of stone, topped with brick walkways and watchtowers, the walls reached toward the clouds, casting a vast shadow on the earth below. No army could scale or shatter them. Within, the city bustled gaily.

The Greeks attempted to force open the gates but suffered grave losses from archers perched above. Next, they endeavored to starve the Trojans, but found they hadn't enough men to both encircle the city and protect their precious fleet. Stalemated, Agamemnon decided to strike at Priam's many allies. City after city up and down the coast was besieged.

Year after year dragged by. Fearless Achilles led most of the raids and brought back to the Greek camp shiploads of treasure. But after eight wearying years, behind Troy's wall, Paris still possessed Helen, the treasure the Greeks had come to claim.

A10   L

Afghan War: In Year Seven, a Deadly Stalemate

By BERNARD E. TRAINOR
Special to The New York Times

WASHINGTON, Feb. 17 — With the Afghan war now in its seventh year, and with serious fighting having ebbed for the winter, neither side appears any closer to winning than they were when Soviet troops joined the fray in December 1979, military experts say.

Military Analysis   The situation is difficult to assess because few qualified, independent observers are permitted into Afghanistan. But despite the uncertainty over details, patterns and trends suggest that the outcome will be in doubt for some time to come.

The war has been costly to the Soviet Union — its forces have reportedly suffered 30,000 casualties — and analysts say the Russians would like to get out of "their Vietnam."

There is no easy way out, however, that does not imply a Soviet defeat, a repudiation of the Brezhnev doctrine and the abandonment of the Soviet-installed Afghan Government under Najib. That doctrine, formulated at the time of the Soviet invasion of Czechoslovakia in 1968, holds that the Soviet Union cannot allow a Communist regime on its borders to be overthrown.

Russians Not Seen Leaving

"If the Americans were fighting the war," an expert on the Soviet Union said, "they would be losing."

He said American frustration with the inconclusiveness of the war would have created domestic pressures to abandon the effort, something that is not the case in the Soviet Union.

So, despite the assessment of the Soviet leader, Mikhail S. Gorbachev, that the Afghan war is a "bleeding wound," and the recent offer of a cease-fire and a phased Soviet withdrawal, it is not likely that the Russians will call it quits in Afghanistan anytime soon.

What is likely for the coming year, according to experts, is that the Soviet Union will seek to improve the military situation with the current force of 115,000 soldiers. Intelligence sources say they do not believe the Russians are willing to commit more troops.

At the same time, the experts say, the Moscow leadership will seek an acceptable political formula that will leave a friendly Afghanistan on the Soviet Union's southern border. According to one Afghan specialist, "The Russians know they can't win militarily, so they are looking for a creative political solution."

Much American intelligence on the war is based on satellite photographs and radio interceptions. Although this results in accurate, quantifiable intelligence on such things as numbers of [...] and troops, it provides little in [...] of insight.

[...]lear on Who Is Ahead

[...]ence of firsthand informa[...] experts differ on which [...] per hand. The State De[...] Pentagon are gen[...]ver battlefield pros[...]rrillas, as long as [...]continue to flow to [...]stan. Many intelli[...] are divided in [...]utside experts

[...]erilla fighters [...]ases since the [...]er of 1979, with [...]inst a new left [...]guerrillas have [...]homeland devas[...]

[...]tas have demon[...]skill in guerrilla [...]own a limited abil-

New tactics beget guerrilla countertactics.

SOVIET UNION

Mazar-i-
Sharif   Kunduz

Herat   Kabul   Jalalabad

Shindand   Ghazni

AFGHANISTAN

Kandahar

PAKISTAN

The New York Times/Feb. 18, 1987

Soviet strategy seems to be to secure the major Afghan cities, connected by the so-called Ring Road.

ity to carry the war to the Soviet-occupied cities. But to date, the guerrillas do not pose a serious threat to the Soviet occupation. Nor have the guerrillas shown more than a marginal willingness to put aside tribal differences and help one another against the Russians and the Kabul Government.

Military experts agree that the performance of the Soviet Army has been generally poor throughout the war, with the exception of special units. Its allied Afghan Army of approximately 30,000 has been known more for desertions than for effectiveness, according to most experts.

Soviet troop morale is reported to be low, and drugs have become a problem. Poor sanitation and hygiene in the field have resulted in a high incidence of sickness such as hepatitis. Even Soviet air supremacy, the Russian strong suit

in the war, is being trumped by the insurgents now that they have received hand-held American Stinger antiaircraft missiles.

About 150 of the heat-seeking missiles were delivered to the guerrillas last year and there are reports that additional ones will be sent soon. According to a Defense Department source, the mujahedeen, as the guerrillas are known, have been quick to learn how to operate the weapon and have had a 70 percent success rate against Soviet planes and helicopters. The source also indicated that morale among Soviet helicopter pilots has become a problem since the appearance of the Stinger on the battlefield.

To avoid embarrassment to Pakistan, United States officials are reluctant to say much about the flow of American military aid that goes to the guerrillas by way of Pakistan. It has been reliably reported, however, that in addition to providing Stingers, the Central Intelligence Agency finances the purchase of Chinese-made arms, which are shipped to the guerrillas through Pakistan.

Sources say that the combination of United States-supplied weapons and those captured from the Russians and the Afghan Army has solved the weapons shortage experienced by the resistance in the early days of the war.

Throughout the last six years, the Russians and the Afghan Army have experimented with strategies and tactics in search of a successful military

antidote to the guerrillas. To date they do not appear to have found it.

At the outset, the Russians tried to leave fighting to the Afghan Army and restricted use of Soviet forces to small-scale forays against the guerrillas. When it became clear that the Afghan Army was no match for the guerrillas and that desertion by Government troops was widespread, the Soviet Army became more actively involved.

There followed large-scale operations and the deliberate destruction of villages and crops, and officers planned combined offensives that made heavy use of bombers, tanks and artillery. But the Russians soon realized that this tactic, suitable for the plains of Central Europe, would not work in mountainous Afghanistan. The guerrillas merely melted into the hills in the face of superior Soviet firepower.

Thereafter, the Russians tried helicopter-borne attacks with regular army units. Special units known as "spetsnaz" were brought in to employ counterguerrilla tactics, and Soviet attack aircraft were introduced to harry the guerrillas and their supply lines from Pakistan.

Each shift in Soviet tactics met with some initial success, but the guerrillas quickly came up with countertactics to frustrate the Russians.

Success, but Not Victory

As successful as the guerrillas have been in defending themselves, however, this cannot be viewed as victory. The guerrillas have hurt the Russians, but they have not defeated them.

To date, guerrilla successes have been of three types. They have frequently ambushed Soviet and Government forces. These include ambushes of Soviet aircraft and helicopters that are lured into valleys only to come under insurgent fire from heavy machine guns and missiles.

The guerrillas have also been successful in disrupting Soviet supply lines. In a land of few roads, most of which wind through the mountains, the guerrillas have trapped and destroyed many supply trucks. In the eastern regions, the Russians can safely move down the roads only in convoys heavily supported by aircraft and helicopters providing covering fire.

The most dramatic and visible guerrilla successes have been in the form of rocket attacks on Government-controlled cities, airfields and supply depots. The Russians have established defensive positions around the most important targets, but the guerrillas still manage to avoid the defenses to launch rockets against targets in Kabul and other heavily defended areas.

But for all their tactical successes, the guerrillas have failed to come up with a strategy that will lead to military victory. Unless they do, military experts say, the initiative remains with the Russians, and six years of experience may allow them to develop a tolerable and potentially successsful long-term strategy.

Evidence of a new and possibly workable Soviet strategy began to emerge last year. The goal of the strategy seems to be to safeguard the major cities in Afghanistan and the routes that connect them with the flow of supplies from the Soviet Union. Offensive operations may be restricted to local pacification efforts around the cities and attacks against guerrilla supply efforts from Pakistan.

The cities to be put under firm Government control are connected by a road that forms a circle around the country and is called the Ring Road by some American military analysts. The cities include Kabul, Ghazni and Jalalabad in the mountainous east; Kunduz and Mazar-i-Sharif, north of the Hindu

Kush mountains; Herat, Shindand a[...] Farah to the desert west, and Kan[...] har in the south.

Control of these cities and the su[...] rounding territory would put much o[...] the population under Government domination. To do this, informed sources say, semiautonomous commands have been established in zones around the country.

The zone commander is a local Afghan of proven ability, who is assisted by Russian advisers. Each zone commander is in a population center and has at his disposal a variety of Afghan units to include the army, the secret police, tribal militias and special light units of Pushtoon warriors called Sarandoy.

In addition, the zones contain Soviet light battalions made up of airborne troops trained for motorized or helicopter operations. Each zone commander is responsible for the pacification of his region with the units assigned and can call upon Kabul for additional help.

The rest of the Soviet and Afghan forces remain under the control of higher headquarters, available for other operations like the reinforcement of zones and the protection of supply lines, airfields and convoys.

With this strategy, the Russians are apparently settling in for a methodical pacification of the populated areas. Military analysts say they believe that top priority is being given to the Kabul region and the area north of the Hindu Kush, astride the three major Soviet supply routes into Afghanistan.

In addition to military pacification efforts, the Russians have also undertaken political, economic and psychological programs to try to convert the Afghans under their control into loyal supporters of the Kabul Government. If they succeed over time, military experts say, the guerrillas will be reduced to a mere nuisance.

WAR

$7[...]

From

The dispirited Greeks grew quick to quarrel, loathed their camp, and longed to go home. Had Prince Palamedes not taken a sheep's knuckle bones and made the first pair of dice, the endless campaign might have driven them mad. All lauded him, save Odysseus. He was jealous of the cleverness that had also led the prince to invent lighthouses, weights and measures, and the alphabet. He'd not forgotten that it was Palamedes who'd forced him to honor his oath and leave Ithaca. When, in the war's ninth year, Palamedes mocked him for leading a failed raid, Odysseus decided: He would endure him no more.

Stealthily, he buried a sack of gold beneath Palamedes' hut. He then produced a forged letter from Priam to Palamedes stating the gold to be payment for betraying the Greeks. Summoned before Agamemnon, the prince swore the letter was false and that he knew nothing of the gold. Odysseus suggested that Palamedes' hut be searched.

A soldier began digging. He soon struck the sack. Agamemnon well remembered the dark days in Aulis, when the army had whispered of making Palamedes its commander. Taking secret pleasure in the sight, he stared at the gold—then condemned the prince to death.

Palamedes was led to a patch of open ground. Soldiers gathered in a ring around him.

"Truth, you have died before me!" he cried.

The men then commenced to stone him.

Jury Is Told That Swaggart Spread Rumors on Rival Out of Jealousy

NEW ORLEANS, July 16 (AP) — The defamation trial of the evangelist Jimmy Swaggart opened today, with the plaintiff's lawyer saying Mr. Swaggart had spread rumors out of jealousy.

The lawyer, Hunter Lundy, told the jury that Mr. Swaggart had felt threatened by the rising popularity of his client, the evangelist Mar... ...r Swaggart was a...

man's ministry by spreading rumors about the preacher's sex life, the lawyer charged.

"Marvin Gorman was not a big-time televangelist," Mr. Lundy told jurors in state civil court here. "He was a pastor trying to use TV to spread the word of God..."

...aggart's lawyer, ...d Mr. Gorman ...er who ... am... ...nan.

Envy Seen As Sensitive Barometer

Along with jealousy, it points to areas where people stake their pride.

By DANIEL GOLEMAN

A GRADUATE student, depressed that his adviser had taken on another student as well, tried to sign up for all the adviser's appointments so there would be no time left for his rival.

A scientist who prided himself on being a prodigy became contemptuous when a close colleague received a MacArthur Foundation "genius" award, saying the prize was based on contacts, not merit.

An executive developed an obsession about another with less experience who was hired for a simi... ...compar... at a higher salary. terms ... ...her woman in attract...

The ... close ... attention ... emerg... sensi... abo... but ... the ... Dr. Univ...

Relationships

Jealousy: Roots of Rage and Revenge

JEALOUSY, one of the most powerful and most perverse of human emotions, has become a central point of contention in a Westchester County murder trial that has attracted nationwide attention.

In the trial, the prosecution is attempting to prove that Jean S. Harris killed Dr. Herman Tarnower in a "jealous rage" over a younger woman who, it contended, had supplanted her in his affections. Mrs. Harris denies the ...tion.

"It is a fact," the prosecutor, ...Bolen, demanded, "that you in... to kill Dr. Tarnower, and then ...self, because if you couldn't ... nobody could."

...r. Bolen, Mrs. Harris re...

...hose closely follow... ...trial are several m... ...sionals with a spec... ...treatment of jealo... ...as Cain and Abel.

...menting direct... ...the professi... ...hological roo... ...re role it pla... ...ships and th... ...channeled...

...confuse of... ...nvy. Both... ...elings"... ...met depe... ...m a real... the m... ...me; I mu... ...ter in s... ...Dr...

The Resentment of Genius

IF YOU are very lucky, life every now and then presents an Answer, a moment of illumination when the veil is lifted and everything — all one's troubles and disappointments — are explained. For me it happened when I least expected it — just this morning as I was reading the Washington Post magazine.

There's a long article about a local girl of 17, Elizabeth Mann, who is a genius. "She is more than smart, in fact. She is brilliant. She scored 1570 (out of 1600) on her SATs, 800 (out of 800) on her Achievement test in math and 800 on her Achievement test in physics. She is a National Merit finalist and a presidential scholar semifinalist, and she was accepted into every college she applied to, finally settling on Harvard." But, adds the reporter, "it's a heavier burden than you think." She was recently at work, for instance, on a physics project exploring "Particle Displacement Velocimetry," but is so advanced that "she couldn't even find somebody to talk to about the wavelet transform." If she dares to use such terms, other kids think she's putting on airs. Misunderstood, mocked by class... ...esented even by teachers, held ...being too precocious, geniuses ...es fraught with special chal- ...says the reporter. All too often, ...re made to fe... ...se serio... ...ss than love in ...ud put it, that envy is a ...a threat to self-esteem. ...n scientists are captur-

...they th... But ho... dow... know... Li... most ... being ... cial a... much ... ward... dete... squ... inn... nor... m... te... cr... a...

Slaying of Soviet Pop Singer Is Laid to Dispute With Rival

MOSCOW, Oct. 7 (Reuters) — The slaying of a popular Soviet singer on Sunday stemmed from a dispute with a rival over who should go on stage first at a concert in St. Petersburg, the official press agency Tass reported today.

The singer, Igor Talkov, was shot to death at the Palace of Sport by an assistant to the rival singer, known as Azizal, Tass quoted a police ...saving. The killer... ...police said.

On Page C12

The news of Palamedes' execution nearly felled his father, King Nauplius. He thought of his son's noble nature and knew that the charge of treason was false. Ablaze with rage, he set sail for Troy.

Landing at the Greek camp, he assailed Agamemnon with questions. He studied the letter that had slain his son and denounced it as a forgery. He accused the Greek generals of a plot but could offer no proof of his claim. Withdrawing his ships and soldiers from Troy, he sailed away, shouting to all that he'd punish his son's foul murderers. It was a promise he fulfilled at once.

Rather than returning home, Nauplius traveled south to Crete, then Ithaca, then Mycenae, and onward, visiting the palaces of all the absent Greek kings. As they'd spread lies about his son, Nauplius now repaid them in kind, informing each queen that her husband planned to replace her with a ravishing captive he'd taken as his new wife.

Desolated by this tale, a few of the women took their own lives. Some took new lovers of their own. Others, while watching for their husbands' ships, made plans to murder their faithless men upon their return from Troy.

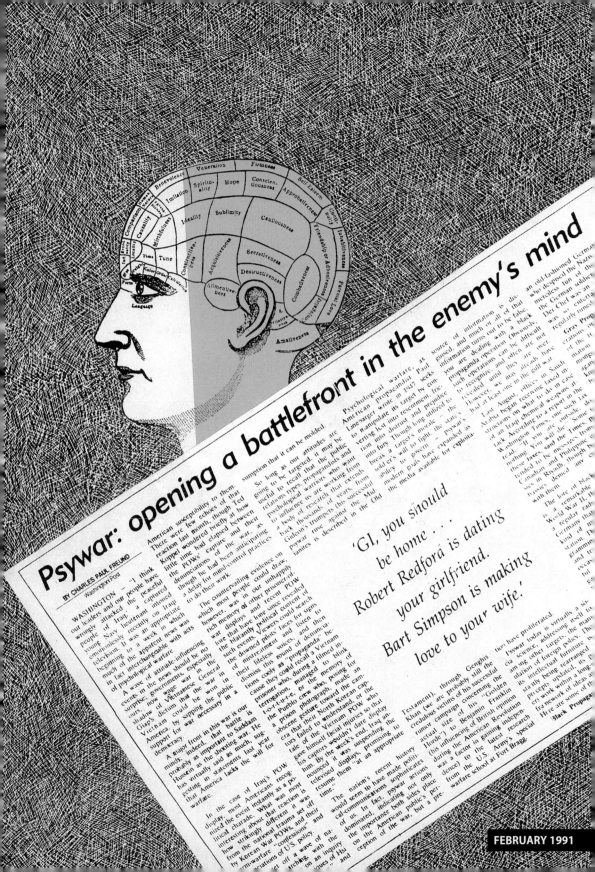

Psywar: opening a battlefront in the enemy's mind

BY CHARLES PAUL FREUND
Washington Post

WASHINGTON — "I think our leaders and our people have wrongly attacked the peaceful people of Iraq," a captured young Navy lieutenant intoned emotionlessly recently on Iraqi television. It was an appropriate beginning to a week in which much of the apparent news was in fact interchangeable with acts of psychological warfare.

A wave of attitude-influencing events in the news should be no surprise; in the shadow of Vietnam, governments—especially ours, now waging war in the shadow of Vietnam. Giap's dictum that the General could be won by sapping the public support for war is as much, suggesting in statements last year that America lacks the will for warfare.

A major front in this war is our minds, indeed; that battle is probably as important to Saddam Hussein as the shooting war. He has virtually said as much, suggesting in statements last year that America lacks the will for warfare.

In the case of Iraq's POW display, most Americans recognized the event instantly as a political charade. What was most interesting about that reaction is how strikingly different it was from the national trauma set off by Korean War POWs, and their germ-warfare "confessions," and recitations of U.S. policy.

The nation's recent history would seem to have made political-communications sophisticates of us. In fact, psywar actions dominated, indicating not only the importance both sides place on the American public's perception of the war, but a pre

'GI, you should
be home . . .
Robert Redford is dating
your girlfriend.
Bart Simpson is making
love to your wife.'

sumption that it can be molded. So long as our attitudes are going to be targeted, it may be useful to recall that the public relations types, propagandists and psychological warriors who want to influence us are working from a body of research that extends back thousands of years, from Gideon's trumpets (his successful psywar ruse against the Midianites is described in the Old

Psychological warfare, as American propagandist Paul Linebarger wrote in 1947 seeks to manipulate its target by converting lust into resentment, friction into distrust and prejudice into fury. Though long utilized to break a target's morale, or the soldier's will to fight, the state's ability to govern — psywar's modern goals have expanded as the media available for exploita

Testament), through Genghis Khan (we are probably still the credulous victims of his successful rumor campaign concerning the actual size of his "Golden Horde") to Benjamin Franklin (his influencing of British opinion during the American Revolution was a factor in gaining independence) to the latest research from the U.S. Army's special warfare school at Fort Bragg.

source of information is disguised, and much or all of that information turns out to be false, you are dealing with a black propaganda operation. Obviously, such operations can be difficult to recognize, and often are not revealed until they are over. However, we may already have had at least one in the Gulf war.

Like Nauplius, Achilles believed Palamedes innocent. Unlike the other Greeks, he wasn't afraid to say so. His love for Palamedes turned to hate for Agamemnon, whose parceling out of captured booty now maddened Achilles past bearing.

"Not once have you risked your life in a raid!" he brazenly condemned the commander. "When have you crouched in the cold half the night, waiting for the moment to attack? What men have you slain? What wounds have you suffered? Yet you take the largest share of the spoils, while we who fight get next to nothing!"

"I take what I'm due!" cried Agamemnon. "I am the High King. Remember it, Achilles! And remember that you're no more than a prince! Now leave my sight at once!"

The Executive Life/Deirdre Fanning

Butlers and Crystal, As Well as a View

Peeled oranges, private jets for dogs and ski lodges. Bosses love their perks.

HEARD the one about the $300 orange? WPP Group P.L.C. did, much to its horror. After it acquired the J. Walter Thompson Company in 1987, the advertising agency discovered that its new acquisition owned an office in New York with an executive dining room that had been excavated from a Colonial New England house, transported to New York and reconstructed at the firm's Lexington Avenue office.

That in itself seemed extravagant. But WPP also found that uniformed butlers routinely took water to the offices of J. Walter Thompson executives in cut-glass crystal decanters on silver trays, and that the dining room's maitre d'hotel stopped by their doors daily to take luncheon orders. Keeping up the two executive floors was costing the firm more than $4 million a year.

•

But perhaps the most egregious excess of the old regime came in the form of a single peeled orange that one of the executives had a butler deliver to him every day. A peeled orange a day, WPP figured, cost the firm about $80,000 a year or, roughly, $300 an orange.

With the intense competition for new accounts, the advertising business has traditionally provided lavish extras for its employees and clients. Although the orange, the dining room and the butlers are now history, the economy weakens and corporate

mer Shear... Naomi Le... who also... nue shop... paneled... West — k... find hom... tives se... boasta... course,... who ac...

Pete... self th... tive fi... was th... Singe... with... men... righ... Te... for...

A4 MONDAY, FEBRUARY 6, 1989

Congressional Benefits Excessive?

Foes Call Some Perks 'Outrageously' Ample

Surveying those benefits and a wealth of others, Claybrook, the president of the Ralph Nader-founded group Public Citizen, said, "The benefits for members of Congress are at least equal to, if not better than, the benefits of the highest-paid executives of the biggest companies in the country."

Among the perks compiled in a Nader report last month that charged that lawmakers' benefits "far exceed the benefits provided to the average American worker":

...lowance: Each mem... expense allowance, ...t of maintaining a ...for 32 round trips a ...r's district and for ...one calls. This ac... ...e used for a range ...nses, from official ...mber and staff to ...upplies, leasing of ...beverages, and ...ers.

...on: Members of ...ecial $3,000 tax ...expenses asso... ...econd residence

...communication: ...s to radio and ...derwritten by ...m messages ...nts, and to ...at a cost of ...r—to keep ...ned.

...ge of other ...ee parking, ...s, U.S. gov... ...rds, banking ...nd passport

...report con... ...and allow... ...ilitate the ...rs. They ...ways the ...ordinarily ...laries of ...compare ...those in

...rs dis... ...Frank ...e side ...second ...r, you

EXECUTIVE PAY
SALARY SCALES

WEDNESDAY, APRIL 18, 1990

CAUGHT IN THE MIDDLE

Managers don't mind that the CEO makes a lot of money, but they raise questions about fairness

By Amanda Bennett

WHEN IT COMES to compensation, w... makes middle managers see red? It isn't that some chief execu... salaries rival those of ballplayers or... stars, or that golden parachutes pro... ate. It isn't that stock options can d... more pay than a middle manager will earn in... time. And it isn't simply that their own pay... seem paltry.

What really makes middle managers... unfairness.

Listen to this vice president and financial analyst at a major bank: "It disturbs me... when someone on high dictates that no... matter how hard you work or what you do,... you're only going to get a 6% increase, and... if you don't like it, you can take a hike. Yet... whatever they've negotiated for them... selves—10% or 20% or 30%—is a different... issue from the rest of the staff." Adds Joe, a... manager at Sterling Drugs Inc.: "It's creat... ing a gap between those who do and those... who have."

Setting Pay Raises

That same bitterness surfaces repeated... in a panel discussion with a group of midd... managers. Ask them about what their CE... makes, and most profess not to know... care. Ask them about their own pay, a... seem particularly bothered...

Marines Probe General's Use of Military Planes

By ERIC LICHTBLAU
TIMES STAFF WRITER

EL TORO—The Marine Corps inspector general Monday launched a formal investigation into whether the commander of the Corps' Western air bases misused military aircraft for personal trips to Big Bear, Florida and elsewhere around the country.

Col. Jim Williams, the Corps' deputy inspector general in Washington, said that after reviewing a report in the Los Angeles Times on Friday, his office decided to open a full investigation of Brig. Gen. Wayne T. Adams, who oversees air bases at El Toro, Tustin, Camp Pendleton and Yuma, Ariz.

The Times article de-tailed five flights either...

FEBRUARY 1989–APRIL 1991

The choicest plunder brought back by the Greeks wasn't fashioned of gold or bronze, but of flesh. Her name was Chryseis. Beholding her beauty, Agamemnon claimed her at once as his slave. He was so enchanted by her shape and her smile that when her father, a priest of Apollo, arrived and begged to buy her freedom, Agamemnon refused the holy man and threatened him with a beating if he returned.

The priest appealed to Apollo for help. Furious with Agamemnon, the god took up his silver bow and rained plague-tipped arrows upon the Greeks. The sickness spread quickly. Men died in hundreds. Day and night the funeral pyres blazed. When Agamemnon demanded that Calchas tell him the cause, the seer feared to answer. Boldly, Achilles vowed to protect him.

"The cause lies with you," Calchas told the king. "You must give up Chryseis, or Apollo will slay us all."

Japan Admits WWII Use of Sex Slaves

Apologies Offered to Captive Asian Women Forced to 'Comfort' Troops

By T. R. Reid
Washington Post Foreign Service

TOKYO, Aug. 4—Moving toward a fuller acceptance of responsibility for its deeds during World War II, the government of Japan conceded today that the Imperial Army forced large numbers of captive Asian women to serve as sex slaves for Japanese soldiers during the war and expressed its "sincere apologies and remorse" to the women and their survivors.

Prime Minister Kiichi Miyazawa's office issued a hastily prepared report admitting that so-called "comfort women" were made to serve as forced prostitutes between 1932 and 1945 in Japan and other Asian nations colonized by Japanese. The government said it would study whether and how to compensate them.

The report was issued on Miyazawa's last day in office, and government officials said he had particularly wanted to act on the issue before his term ended.

But the newly elected coalition government taking office Thursday has promised to go much further than Miyazawa's or any previous postwar government in taking the blame for World War II war crimes and apologizing to the victims.

For decades, Japanese governments have been criticized at home and abroad for failing to face up to the country's responsibility for acts of brutality in East Asia and the Pacific before and during the war.

Japanese emperors and prime ministers had issued statements of regret in recent years, but they never used the word "apologize." Thus there remains a str...
in Asia th...

ing back. History textbooks and classes here cover the war crimes, but generally in a perfunctory way. Many Japanese students are stunned when they learn the full extent of Asia's lingering anger.

Leaders of the new coalition government have vowed to change that. "It think . . . the right thing to do is to offer a clear apology," said Tsutomu Hata, a leader of the coalition who is likely to be vice prime minister of the new government.

"We need at long last to take a soul-searching look at the meaning of the war," he said this week. "We

See TOKYO, A22, Col. 1

Squ
■ Bo
close
key de
point f
govern
defendi
WORLD,

Md. C

■ Maryla
president
to investig
awarding
saying the
system is a
METRO, *Pag*

■ Private and
economists s

Contents

"Wretch!" exploded Agamemnon at Calchas. "Your prophecies bring me only grief!" Afraid, however, that Calchas was right, he agreed to return the girl, but declared he'd replace her with a slave of his choosing, one equally as attractive: Achilles' handmaiden, Briseis.

"Greedy, dog-faced thief!" spoke Achilles. "You recruit me to fight, then rob me of my spoils! You're no better than a brigand! I owe you no service. I swore no oath to Menelaus. Let the Trojans overrun the camp and drive spears through your haughty heart! I'm going home!"

"Be off then, coward!" shouted Agamemnon. "I won't beg you to stay, or miss your insolence. But be warned that my heralds will visit you this day. And as certain as I am the High King of the Greeks, you'll give them your fair Briseis."

Achilles yanked his sword from its sheath.

Leafs Fall to Rangers

John Ogrodnick of the Rangers watching
blocked his shot in the first period at the Gard
other chance and helped the Rangers to a 7-4 vic

Strawberry Threatens To Leave Camp

By JOSEPH DURSO
Special to The New York Times

PORT ST. LUCIE, Fla., March 1 — The
comparative calm of the Mets' camp was
shattered today when Darryl Strawberry
carried his campaign for a new contract
into a new dimension by threatening to
walk out "if they don't have this worked out
by tomorrow."

"He's under contract for the next two
years," replied Al Harazin, senior vice
president of the Mets, "and we'll talk about
extending it but not about renegotiating it.
And if he's not working out in camp, if he's
in breach of his contract, we won't even
talk."

chschmidt of
meeting
morn-
work-

out,
ng of
he re-

"I will be at practice on time tomorrow.
If it's not a positive meeting, there's no telling how long I'll be on the field. It's a disgrace to me and my family that I might

---

He says he'll walk out if the Mets don't satisfy his contract demands.

---

have to walk out. But I think my teammates
will understand."

His teammates did not understand entire-
ly. They saluted him as the team's biggest
home-run hitter and most important
player, but they also questioned the wisdom
of a walkout.

"You got to get what you deserve," said
Dwight Gooden, who signed a three-year
contract recently for $6.7 million. "Darryl's
got to get paid. But he

A billboard at the side of a highway in Dal

Coaching C Is Still the

But Jimmy Johnson

By GERALD ESKENAZI
Special to The New York Times

IRVING, Tex., March 1 — The walls of
Jimmy Johnson's office are bare, except
for a few hooks left where Tom Landry
had removed 29 years of memories. But
it's Johnson's room now, and Johnson's
Dallas Cowboys football team.

"I feel so much better today," the new
coach said this morning. He already had
a draft list on his table, had looked at
films, had spoken to players, and was por-
ing over phone numbers of potential
assistants to call.

The emotion of Tuesday's first news
conference, at which he fended off hostile
questions, appears to have shifted. The
45-year-old Johnson finally permitted
himself to show his p
merely being defe
legacy.

"You come here and want to be head
coach of the Dallas Cow

MARCH 1989

Instantly, Athena alit. Visible only to Achilles, she clutched his arm and turned him from bloodshed. "Do not sail home," she counseled him. Athena well knew that Achilles was vital to her goal of punishing Paris and the Trojans. He submitted to her, but swore that he'd not raise his sword against Troy. Then he strode away.

Chryseis was put on a ship and sent home. Agamemnon then ordered two heralds to Achilles' hut to seize Briseis. They entered in fear. Achilles' eyes smoldered. Obedient to Athena's wishes, he gave up the girl peaceably, then stalked off in a rage toward the shore. He called out to his sea goddess mother, who rose up at once from her undersea cave and heard all the indignities he'd suffered. Burning to humble Agamemnon, she carried her son's lament to Zeus and so badgered him that he at last agreed to punish the proud High King. That very night he did so.

While Agamemnon was sleeping, Zeus sent him a deceitful dream. Agamemnon awoke before dawn. Hurriedly, he called his council.

"Put on your armor!" he ordered them. "Zeus has spoken to me in a dream. Today he will allow us to conquer the Trojans! Ready the men to march!"

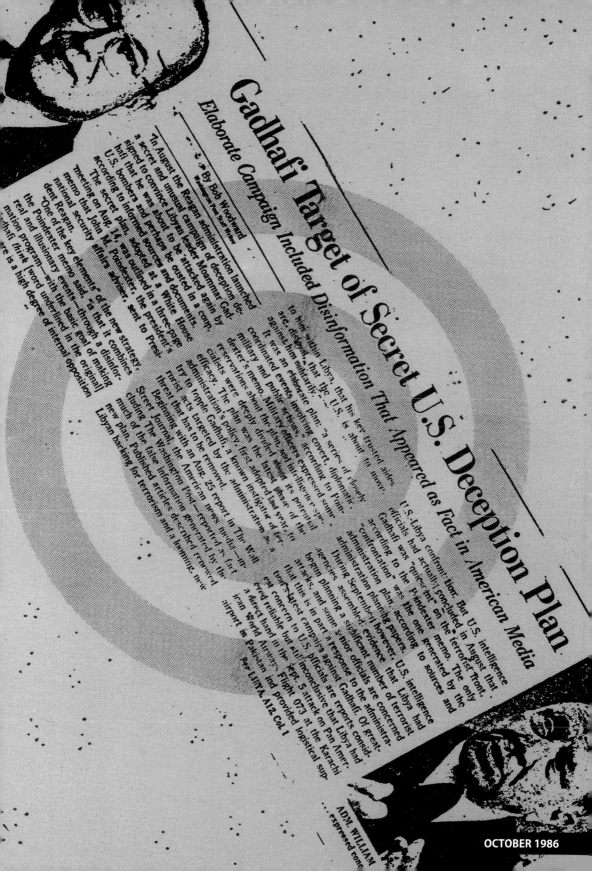

The Greeks marched out, all but Achilles and his men. Pouring through their gates came the Trojans. The two armies met, spears whistling, swords slashing. The plain before Troy was soon strewn with dead. Then Hector, Priam's eldest son and Troy's greatest warrior, called for both sides to halt. His brother Paris, he shouted out, would stop the slaughter by fighting Menelaus. The winner would be granted Helen, settling the matter and ending the war. A truce was declared. The grateful soldiers sat in long lines to watch the combat.

The rivals approached. Both flung their spears, Menelaus wounding Paris. The Spartan king then raised his sword and shattered it upon Paris' helmet. The Trojan staggered. Left without a weapon, Menelaus grabbed Paris' helmet and dragged him toward the Greek lines in triumph. Seeing Paris being strangled by his chin strap, Aphrodite, his protector, caused it to snap, sending Menelaus sprawling. Menelaus jumped up, determined to kill Paris—and gaped to find him gone. Aphrodite had made him invisible and had whisked him to safety within Troy.

"Bring forth Helen!" demanded Menelaus. It was clear to both sides that he was the victor. "Send her out through the gates!"

Watching from Olympus, Hera and Athena were aghast at the prospect of peace. To punish Paris for awarding the golden apple to Aphrodite, they'd wanted more than Helen's return. Troy, they'd resolved, must be destroyed. Fearing the Greeks would claim Helen and sail home, Athena disguised herself as a son of Priam and instructed a Trojan to shoot an arrow at Menelaus. A moment later a cry rose from the Greeks. The man had taken aim and wounded Menelaus, basely breaking the truce. Outraged, the Greeks grabbed their weapons. The two armies flew at each other afresh.

Bombings in Beirut: What Was the Motive?

Disruption of Peace Parley Is Termed Terrorists' Goal

By IHSAN A. HIJAZI
Special to The New York Times

BEIRUT, Lebanon, Oct. 23 — Some Lebanese officials asserted today that the terrorist explosions here that killed scores of United States marines and French paratroopers this morning were aimed at undermining the planned peace conference of the country's religious and political factions.

"Every time we make some headway, evil elements act to set us back by killing and destruction," Prime Minister Shafik al-Wazzan told reporters as he joined President Amin Gemayel and other officials in an emergency Cabinet session.

Others, such as former Prime Minister Saeb Salam, a key figure in the peace conference, said the attacks appeared primarily to be an effort to compel the withdrawal of the international force of United States, French, Italian and British troops.

Butros Harb, a member of Parliament and former Cabinet minister, said the deaths of the American and French soldiers had poisoned the political atmosphere and overshadowed the reconciliation process.

Political Effects Discussed

The state-controlled Beirut radio said the Cabinet in its emergency session today discussed the political implications of the bomb attacks against the marines and French troops.

While no evidence is yet available as to who may have been responsible for today's explosions, believed to have been caused by pickup trucks laden with huge quantities of explosives, accusations have been made.

The Christian Phalangist Voice of Lebanon radio said Syria and the Palestinians were to blame. The radio referred to an intensification of criticism of the United States in the state-controlled informational organs in Damascus and a declaration by an official of the Palestine Liberation Organization that preceded the violence today. The P.L.O. official said the multinational force must be withdrawn.

Today's explosions, which destroyed buildings used by units of the multinational force, one at the Marines' headquarters at Beirut International Airport, the other at the French headquarters, came as President Gemayel was preparing for the peace conference scheduled to begin in Switzerland at end of this month.

Parley to Start Oct. 31

According to Lebanese press reports and a statement in Bern by the Foreign Ministry, the Government-sponsored meeting of Lebanese Christian and Moslem delegations is to open in a Geneva hotel on Oct. 31. An effort to open the talks last Thursday in the Beirut Airport failed after the principal participants

American Marines and the Lebanese Army. The decision to hold the conference was part of the overall Lebanese cease-fire accord reached Sept. 26.

In Syria, a commentary broadcast on the Damascus radio today said that United States policy in the area was doomed to failure, but made no reference to the deaths of the French and American troops.

The radio commentary went on to say that American pressures on Syria would compel the Syrians to act to preserve their interests in the Arab world.

On Saturday, a Syrian Government newspaper, responding to President Reagan's remarks at a news conference last Wednesday, at which he accused Syria of obstructing the peace process in Lebanon, warned that Syrian troops in Lebanon had standing orders to retaliate in strength if attacked.

The article, in the newspaper Tichrin, said that Soviet-made surface-to-air missiles now in Syria's possession would not differentiate between American and Israeli jets flying over Syrian positions.

Some analysts here said the way the explosions were carried out today was similar to the manner in which the United States Embassy here was blown up last April 18. Sixteen Americans and more than 50 Lebanese were killed when a terrorist drove a car laden with high explosives into the embassy compound in West Beirut.

Druse Leader Condemns Attacks

PARIS, Oct. 23 (Reuters) — The Lebanese Druse leader, Walid Jumblat, condemned today's attacks on the international force as "tragic."

"I have nothing to do with this affair," he said in an interview in Amman, the Jordanian capital, with Radio France international. "But the military approach, from whichever side, is not the way to solve the Lebanese problem. There must be a political solution."

Mr. Jumblat said a withdrawal by the French contingent in the multinational force in Beirut could have severe effects.

"It's possible that the withdrawal of the French contingent, because it occupies certain strategic positions, especially in giving confidence to the Lebanese and Palestinian refugee population, would be disastrous," he declared.

"The presence of the Americans is another matter," he said. "But in any case I condemn these two attacks,"

Swiss Announce Conf...

THE FRENCH BARRACKS: A French paratrooper, abo... French troops, which collapsed after terrorist attack yesterd...

OCTOBER 1983

Agamemnon's men hurled the Trojans back, stripping the bloody bodies of their armor. King Diomedes slew more than any other, driving his spear between the eyes of the Trojan who'd injured Menelaus. He even stabbed the war god Ares, who'd been watching the carnage with delight. Howling, the god fled to Olympus.

Hector dashed back to Troy seeking Paris and found him resting in Helen's chamber. "Coward!" he bellowed. He roughly led him out, took leave of his own weeping wife and tiny son, and sped back to the battle, crying a challenge to the Greeks to send a warrior to oppose him.

His words brought the fighting to a stop. Agamemnon's generals eyed Hector in dread, knowing Achilles alone could defeat him. Unable to decide who should go forth, they at last cast lots. Each man put a marked pebble into a helmet. The helmet was shaken. All waited. Then out jumped the stone belonging to Ajax, the biggest of the Greeks.

Variably cloudy tod
Mostly cloudy tonight, tomorrow
Temp. range: today 35-24; Mond.
40-33. Full U.S. report on Page ?

APPROVES
LLOWANCE
AX TO 23%

imum Figure
e With 20%
Endorsed

ANAHAN
ork Times
ec. 1—The
to reduce
ace for oil
o 23 per
that the
rrent tax
se allow-
vel.
is be-
e first
ongress
allow-
cent
into

eady
e to
of
be
use
ill
at
e

ONE OF THE FIRST DRAWS: Paul M. Murray, 18, a member of President Nixon's Youth Advisory Council, taking one of the capsules out of the cylinder. Col. Daniel Omar, seated, announces the birthdates as Col. Charles Fox posts the information on board at right.

United Press International

LOTTERY IS HELD TO SET THE ORDER OF DRAFT IN 1970

First Birth Dates Selected Are Sept. 14, April 24, Dec. 30 and Feb. 14

850,000 ARE AFFECTED

Each Is Assigned a Number —Top Third of the List Is Likely to Be Called

By DAVID E. ROSENBAUM
Special to The New York Times

WASHINGTON, Dec. 1—The futures of young men across the country were decided tonight as, one by one, the dates of their births were drawn in the first draft lottery in a generation.

Shortly after 8 P.M., Representative Alexander Pirnie of Utica, N. Y., reached into a large glass bowl and pulled out a blue capsule. The capsule was opened, and the date was read—Sept. 14.

Representatives of the Selective Service System's Youth Advisory Committees then drew the remaining 365 dates, and each date was posted on a board. The drawing was completed by 9:30.

All Who Have Not Served

In dormitories and living rooms young men and their families huddled in front of television sets and radios, which intermittently broadcast the order of drawing, to find out how they had fared.

The lottery affected every man in the country between the ages of 19 and 26 who had not served in the military. Each of these men was given a number.

Those whose birthday is Sept.

BACKERS OF NIXON WIN A HOUSE TEST

ongressmen Bar Changes
n Resolution Supporting
Policies on Vietnam

By JOHN W. FINNEY
Special to The New York Times
ASHINGTON, Dec. 1—With
istration encouragement,
ouse began consideration
of a resolution support-
sident Nixon's efforts to
te a "just peace" in

Order of the Draft Drawing

WASHINGTON, Dec. 1—Following is the order in which
birth dates were drawn tonight in the draft lottery:

Special to The New York Times

1	Sept. 14	35	May 7	69	June 13	101	Jan. 5
2	April 24	36	Aug. 24	70	Dec. 21	102	Aug. 15
3	Dec. 30	37	May 11	71	Sept. 10	103	May 30
4	Feb. 14	38	Oct. 30	72	Oct. 12	104	June 19
5	Oct. 18	39	Dec. 11	73	June 17	105	Dec. 8
6	Sept. 6	40	May 3	74	April 27	106	Aug. 9
7	Oct. 26	41	Dec. 10	75	May 19	107	Nov. 16
8	Sept. 7	42	July 13	76	Nov. 6	108	March 1
9	Nov. 22	43	Dec. 9	77	Jan. 28	109	June 23
10	Dec. 6	44	Aug. 16	78	Dec. 27	110	June 6
11	Aug. 31	45	Aug. 2	79	Oct. 31	111	Aug. 1
12	Dec. 7	46	Nov. 11	80	Nov. 9	112	May 17
13	July 8	47	Nov. 27	81	April 4	113	Sept. 15
14	April 11	48	Aug. 8	82	Sept. 5	114	Aug. 6
15	July 12	49	Sept. 3	83	April 3	115	July 3
16	Dec. 29	50	July 7				

DECEMBER 1969

The two heroes met. They heaved their spears, then boulders heavy as millstones, but each man withstood the other's blows. They fought past the setting of the sun. When night fell, heralds raised their sacred staffs and halted the contest. Each warrior richly praised the other. As proof of their respect, the two exchanged gifts: Ajax bestowed his crimson belt, Hector his silver-studded sword. Neither knew that the gifts he received would figure in his own death.

Both sides spent a day burying the fallen. The Greeks laid theirs in a line before their camp, covered them with a great mound of dirt, then faced this earthen wall with stone, using the dead to protect the living.

Boldly, they marched forth the next day—then stopped, fearstruck, at the sight of Mound Ida beyond Troy. Lightning was flickering above it. All knew this meant Zeus would favor the Trojans, who now charged ferociously over the plain. The panicked Greeks fled. Hundreds were speared or crushed underneath chariot wheels.

The Trojan army's campfires blazed just outside the Greeks' wall that night. Realizing Zeus opposed him, Agamemnon was ready to sail home. King Diomedes condemned his cowardice, shaming him into staying on. In desperation Agamemnon humbled himself before Achilles, offering horses, slaves, gold, and even Briseis if only he would fight. Achilles proudly refused.

The next morning, the Greeks pushed back their foes, then were overwhelmed and retreated wildly through the gates in their wall. The Trojans began to scale it. Hefting an enormous boulder, Hector flung it at the gates. They burst open.

"To the ships!" he called out. "Set them afire!"

Brandishing torches, the Trojans poured through the passage and fought their way to the fleet. The desperate Greeks found their backs to the sea. There came the crackle of burning wood. The first plume of smoke rose through the sky.

MAY 1940

Into Achilles' hut burst Patroclus, his cherished friend and cousin. "The first row of ships is in flames!" he shouted. "If you won't fight, at least lend me your armor. The sight of it might save the fleet."

Achilles agreed. Patroclus put it on and led Achilles' men in a charge. The Trojans recognized the shield at once. In terror, sure the invincible Achilles had emerged, they scattered and fled the Greek camp. Patroclus pursued them all the way to Troy, where Hector met him in the midst of the fray. The pair of warriors wrestled like lions, while spears and stones flew past their heads. Another Trojan then wounded Patroclus. Catching him dazed and unguarded, Hector speared him through the belly.

The fight for the body was more savage still. Hector at last stripped it of Achilles' armor and discovered he'd not killed Achilles after all. Bravely, Menelaus rescued Patroclus' corpse and bore it back to the Greek camp.

All dreaded telling Achilles. When he set eyes on the mangled body, he raised a howl that was heard for miles. All night he wept, shrieking his promise to slay his dead friend's slayer.

Thetis heard him, flew to Olympus, and begged Hephaestus, the smith of the gods, to fashion her son new armor. All night he labored with hammer and tongs. At dawn Thetis entered Achilles' hut with such arms and armor as no man had known. The brass helmet was of unsurpassed strength. The breastplate shone brighter than fire. The five-layered shield showed myriad scenes rendered in silver, gold, and gemstones.

Achilles buckled on the armor. He took up his spear and slid his sword in his sheath. Then he bolted outside, ready for revenge.

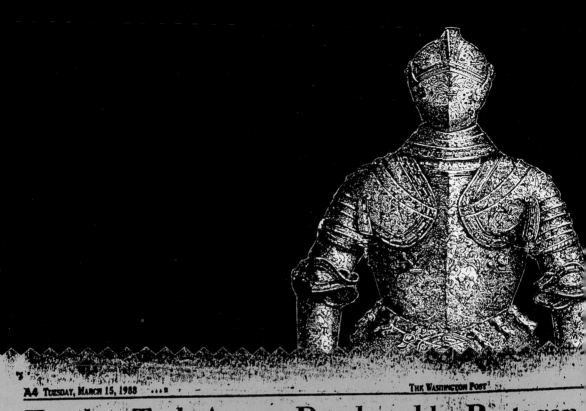

A4 TUESDAY, MARCH 15, 1988   THE WASHINGTON POST

Tougher Tank Armor Developed by Pentagon

Officials Say Plating of Uranium Encased in Steel Is Impervious to Warsaw Pact Weapon

By George C. Wilson
Washington Post Staff Writer

The United States has developed a new tank armor made from a uranium byproduct that is impervious to any Soviet antitank weapon, the Pentagon said yesterday.

The officials said beginning in October, new Army M1 Abrams tanks will be equipped with the armor, made from a mesh of "depleted" uranium encased in steel. It is 2½ times as dense as steel.

Pentagon officials estimated it would take the Soviet Union "almost a decade" to duplicate the new armor plate.

"It's really a major advance," said Pentagon spokesman Fred S. Hoffman in summarizing the secret briefings he received on the new armor.

Not only will the armor plate stop the Soviet antitank missiles in use today, Pentagon officials said, it also cannot be penetrated by those known to be under development. However, the new armor is likely to

spur Soviet development of new antitank weapons, perhaps using depleted uranium shells.

The claimed advance in armor plate comes at a time when the Reagan administration is trying to assure NATO allies that the United States will upgrade its conventional defenses as short- and medium-range nuclear missiles are with-

> ## "It's really a major advance."
> — Pentagon spokesman Fred S. Hoffman

drawn from Europe under the Intermediate-Range Nuclear Forces (INF) Treaty.

Pentagon officials said the development of the armor is evidence of the soundness of the U.S. strategy of offsetting the superior numerical strength of Warsaw Pact troops with higher quality weapons.

They conceded that some Euro-

pean countries, where the tanks will be based, voiced concern over radiation, but the officials said they have allayed those worries.

Depleted uranium, essentially what is left over after uranium is turned into an enriched product for weapons or nuclear reactors, gives off radiation in such small amounts that it endangers nothing, the Pentagon said. The army started briefing factory workers yesterday and issued statements to the news media in an effort to avoid environmental backlash against its new armor.

The army does not intend to issue an environmental impact statement on the use of depleted uranium on M1 tanks, according to spokesman Maj. Phil Soucy, "because we're not required to."

"While depleted uranium has a low level of natural radiation," the Pentagon said, "our tests have confirmed that this material as installed in the Abrams will involve no appreciable health threat. You would re-

ceive less radiation sitting on th[e] surface of that tank than you wou[ld] receive when flying during a tran[s]-Atlantic flight. Because of this lo[w] exposure, no special precaution[s] are required when near the tank."

Soucy said the army is fabricati[ng] the depleted uranium "component[s]" at "classified" facilities that would not identify under a licen[se] issued by the Nuclear Regulato[ry] Commission. The armor plating a[nd] parts will arrive at General Dyna[m]ics' plants in Detroit and Lim[a,] Ohio, with the depleted urani[um] mesh already encased in steel.

The Pentagon would not rev[eal] how much the armor would add [to] the cost of the M1 tank, which n[ow] costs $2.6 million each. It said [the] armor would add some weight [to] the tank but not enough to kee[p it] from achieving its maximum sp[eed] of 42 miles an hour. The army installed a speed regulator to p[re]vent drivers from exceeding t[hat] speed.

The army already has bou[ght]

With a thunderous shout, Achilles woke the Greeks and bid them make ready for battle. Agamemnon, elated to see him, sent to his hut Briseis and the other gifts he'd offered. Achilles took no notice. He could think of nothing but Hector.

The Greeks marched out. The Trojans met them and fell in hundreds before Achilles' spear. Seeing his soldiers in full retreat, Priam opened Troy's gates to them. All entered but Hector, who stood fast outside. Weeping, tearing out his white hair, Priam begged his son to seek safety. Hector refused, heard the gates shut, then saw Achilles advancing and ran. Achilles gave chase. Four times they circled Troy. At last Hector stopped and threw his spear. It rebounded off his foe's divine shield. Achilles then raised his own spear and with the sum of his strength drove it through Hector's neck. Down to the ground crashed the pride of Troy.

"Give my body to my father and mother," Hector pleaded as he died.

"Never!" screamed Achilles. He stripped Hector of his armor. Maddened with grief for Patroclus, he pierced Hector's feet behind his heel tendons, threaded through the belt Ajax had given him, tied it to his chariot, and dragged Hector's body through the dirt, around and around the walls of Troy. In horror, Priam and Hecuba turned their heads from the sight.

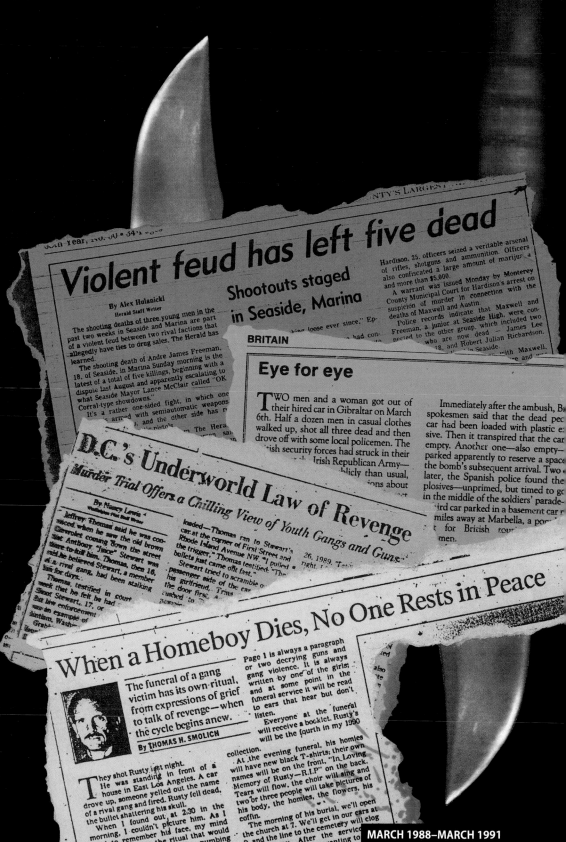

MARCH 1988–MARCH 1991

Achilles trailed Hector's body all the way back to the Greek camp. There he saw to Patroclus' funeral, sending out scores of woodcutters and building a vast pyre of logs one hundred feet square. The flames lit up the land for miles. Achilles made sacrifices and held funeral games, and each dawn afterward he dragged Hector's corpse three times around Patroclus' tomb.

Achilles' behavior so repelled the gods that at last Thetis urged him to return the body. That night, Priam entered his hut in secret, kissed the hands that had slain his son, and begged Achilles to accept the body's weight in gold as a ransom. The anger left Achilles' heart. He knew that his own death was drawing close, that his coming to Troy had fated him for a short, glorious life. Both men wept.

The next day, they met in Apollo's temple. The corpse, washed and clothed in soft linen, was laid upon one pan of a scale. Priam heaped his gold on the other. He hadn't enough. Then his daughter Polyxena stepped forward and added her heavy gold necklace. Slowly, the pan of gold sank down.

WORLD NEWS

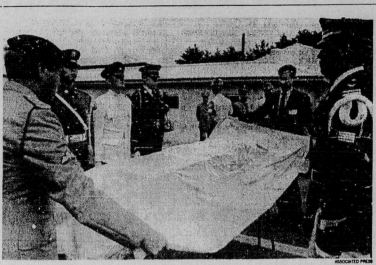

ASSOCIATED PRESS

U.N. soldiers drape flag over coffin holding remains of American killed in Korean War and returned yesterday.

Somber Ceremony at Korean Border

Pyongyang Returns Remains of 5 U.S. Soldiers on Memorial Day

By Peter Maass
Special to The Washington Post

PANMUNJOM, Korea, May 28—Thomas Gregory worked and waited a long time to witness today's Memorial Day ceremony in this truce border village. The Korean War veteran watched as North Korean officials, for the first time in 36 years, turned over the remains of some American soldiers to a U.S. delegation.

American observers saluted and placed their hands over their hearts as 12 North Koreans slowly passed five pine coffins over the border dividing North Korea and South Korea, into the white-gloved hands of a military honor guard.

Rep. G.V. "Sonny" Montgomery (D-Miss.), who headed the American delegation, promised a hero's welcome in the United States for the remains of the five soldiers and called today's ceremony "historic."

"We certainly hope this will open the door for more American remains to come back home for proper burial," said Montgomery, chairman of the House Veterans Affairs Committee. The five sets of remains will be flown to Hawaii for positive identification by forensic experts, he said.

For Gregory, who has lobbied intensively for the return of soldiers' remains from North Korea, today's ceremony was a watershed event.

"I felt a flood of emotion when I watched these guys cross that line," said Gregory, who heads the POW-MIA committee of the Chosin Few, a Korean War veterans organization. Gregory, wounded during the famous retreat from the Chosin Reservoir in North Korea, said after the ceremony that he planned to call relatives of the fallen soldiers.

"It will be an emotional call," Gregory said in a wavering voice. "I am going to say to them that I am very glad to have played a part in bringing their loved ones home."

Today's transfer of the remains was the first by North Korea since a year after the 1950-53 Korean War. The Pentagon lists 33,629 Americans killed during the conflict, nearly as many as during the much longer Vietnam War, and the remains of 8,172 of the dead are still unaccounted for in the rugged hills and tranquil rice paddies of North Korea.

North Korea found the remains returned today—and two sets of dog tags and personal effects including shoes and jackets—in 1987. But Pyongyang delayed a scheduled 1988 transfer of the remains because the United States had placed North Korea on a list of countries sponsoring terrorism. The two countries do not have diplomatic relations.

North Korea has one of the world's last hard-line Communist regimes, and it is coming under pres-

See REMAINS, A20, Col. 3

Myanmar Opposition

Ruling Junta Vows to

By Jeremy Wagstaff
Reuter

YANGON, Myanmar, May 28—The military government of Myanmar, formerly Burma, conceded today that the main opposition party was winning National Assembly elections with two-thirds of the vote and said it would hand over power after parliament agreed on a new constitution.

Foreign governments and opposition leaders had said before Sunday's elections that the army, which brutally crushed an uprising against the military government in September 1988, would try to delay handing over power.

Officials of the junta's information committee told a news conference that the military would play no role in drafting or approving the constitution. The officials did not say how long the process would take but Western diplomats said it could last as long as two years.

"If we had no intention of handing over power, we would not have had these elections," said Soe Nyunt of the ruling State Law and Order Restoration Council.

The multi-party elections Sunday were the first in Myanmar in 30 years, and diplomats said the voting was held fairly and freely despite months of intimidation and harassment of opposition candidates by government officials. The nation's leading opposition figures have been under arrest—including two from the main opposition group, the National League for Democracy—and were barred from contesting the election.

International human rights groups said before the elections that human rights violations were so widespread and restrictions on political expression so severe in Myanmar that a free and fair election was impossible.

The country's military leaders killed at least 1,000 people in the 1988 crackdown on a democracy

---

Nobody Flies

Nonsto
to fly. And o
gives you no
Baltimore/W

MAY 1990

USAir. With

Achilles stared at Polyxena. It was in this same temple, located on neutral ground and used by both Trojans and Greeks, that he'd first set eyes on her weeks before and had fallen instantly in love. His ardor still blazed brightly. He opened his heart to Priam, who promised his daughter in marriage if Achilles could sway the Greeks to leave Helen in Troy. Achilles, made a traitor by passion, swore to do all he could. He was unaware that Polyxena had vowed to avenge her brother Hector's death.

When they met one night, he revealed the secret of his vulnerable right heel to her. The next day, he returned to the temple to meet Priam. Hiding behind a pillar crouched Paris, who suddenly sprang out. He drew his bow, shot a poisoned arrow, and exulted to see it find its mark—Achilles' unprotected heel.

LOVE BLINDNESS

MISTAKES THAT CAN HAUNT YOUR RELATIONSHIP

WE ALL WANT TO BE HAPPY IN love; we want our relationships to work. Yet we often encounter problems—not because either partner is behaving badly but because we made mistakes in choos... mistakes that can detract from a rela... ship for months or even years. ...e beginning of a relationship is th... ...ial time. So much disappointm... be avoided if we just *paid m*... ...at the start.

tionship; it may also he... ou analyze the relationship you're in ...now.

WE DON'T A... ...OUGH QUESTIONS

Think ab... ...a new car. You visit vari... ...looking over the s... ...on, ...denly you spot... ...at real... ...you're in lov... ...ay it looks... ...leather ...er's seat, th... ...spot... ...ap-... ...and feels. A... ...this... ...ches, you exclaim... ..."Let... ..."Well, great," he... ...you about its mile... ...his car." ..."No," you say. ...some ex-... "Well, let me tell... ...safety featur... ...ust ruin ...n s...

Former Girlfriend Charged in Stabbing

Herald Salinas Bureau

SALINAS — A 27-year-old Salinas man allegedly was stabbed with a knife by his former girlfriend in hi... apartment Tuesday...

278

Md. Woman Is Indicted In Murder-for-Hire Plot

By Victoria Churchu...
Washington Post St...

A 50-year-old G... man, who alleged... representative... service to kill... was indicted... gomery... charges o... murder... maim...

picion from herself and McCarthy, the police reports said.

She allegedly told McCarthy that patients under psychiatric care at the hospital routinely threatened to kill her former husband and, if he ...ied, a patient likely would be ac-... police records state. McCar-... to consider Blosser's ... touch with her, ...rds.

...ported Blos-... ...ce kept in

Glen Burnie Woman Charged In Hired Killing of Husband

By Tom V...

ANNAPOLIS, July 6 — A 25-year-old Glen Burnie waitress whose husband was gunned down in a parking lot last week has been arrested and charged with murder for allegedly hiring three men to carry out the slaying, Anne Arundel County police said today.

The three suspected of perform-ing the killing also are in custody on murder charges.

Michael K. Boyd, 25, was shot at 10 p.m. Thursday in the parking lot of his apartment building and died at North Arundel Hospital... later.

Police spokesman... Molloy said Jody... three young child... gators after... her husband... the children...

But Molloy sai...
...been able to...

SEPTEMBER 1984–SEPTEMBER 1992

Odysseus and Ajax had followed Achilles in secret and now rushed into the temple. Valiantly fighting off Trojans, Ajax bore the body away while Odysseus protected him.

The Greeks were bewildered by the news of Achilles' treachery and death. His body was burned, the flames quenched with wine, and his ashes mixed with those of Patroclus and buried in an urn of gold. Thetis then declared that his wondrous armor should go to the bravest of the Greeks. In scorn, she assigned Agamemnon the role of judge rather than candidate. Ajax, the mightiest Greek warrior remaining, felt certain the armor would be his. Instead, Agamemnon chose Odysseus.

The news staggered Ajax. Frenzied with disappointment, he made up his mind: He would kill Agamemnon and Odysseus. He set off that night, sword in hand. Desperate to spare the Greeks' leaders, Athena struck Ajax mad and led him astray. He turned his feet toward the Greek flocks, hacking down goats and sheep by the hundreds, convinced he was killing his enemies. When he rose the next morning, the madness was gone. Slaughtered animals covered the plain, his own body caked with their blood. Astounded, sickened, unable to bear his shame, he took the sword Hector had given him and fixed it to the ground. Then he plunged upon the point.

Student Kills 4, Then Himself at Iowa Campus

■ Crime: The gunman, a native of China, was upset about not receiving an academic honor. Two other persons were wounded in the shootings.

From Associated Press

IOWA CITY, Iowa—A student upset about not getting an academic honor shot four persons to death Friday at the University of Iowa before fatally shooting himself, a school official said. The dead included faculty members and the student who had won the honor.

Two others were critically wounded, authorities said.

The gunman was identified as Gang Lu, a graduate student in physics from China. Ann Rhodes, vice president of university affairs, said. He had filed a complaint with the school's academic affairs office because his dissertation was not nominated for an academic award, she said.

Lu shot three members of the school's physics and astronomy departments and another graduate student in one classroom, then went to the administration building and shot an associate vice president for academic affairs and a staff member. Rhodes said.

Rhodes said that Lu apparently had decided ahead of time whom he was going to shoot.

"It was not accidental," she said. "It was not random."

[Tw]o persons were hospitalized [in critical] condition, Rhodes said. [Lu killed] four people at

Student wounded by gunman in a shooting spree is taken from a building at the University o[f...]

Van Allen Hall, which houses the physics department, then went to Jessup Hall, the administration building, and shot two more people before killing himself, Rhodes said. The gunman was found in Jessup Hall about 10 minutes after the last shootings.

The rampage lasted about 10 minutes, police said.

Iowa City Police Chief R. J. Winkelhake said that police recovered a .38-caliber revolver. Police found the gunman alive, but with fatal head wounds, he said.

Scott Wollenweber, a graduate student, was conducting a review session Friday afternoon for astronomy students in Van Allen Hall.

"It scares the hell out of me," Wollenweber said [...] there the wh[...] students s[...] here i[...]

[of] what sounded like shots."

Mark Lawrence, a graduate student in geography, was attending a seminar in Jessup Hall when he heard a loud noise.

"A very short time later, a cop really burst into the room and simply tells us, 'Get on the floor, turn off the lights, close the door.' and then vanishes," Lawrence said. "We have no idea what's going on."

The shooting occurred less than three weeks after George Jo Hennard drove his truck through the front window of a cafeteria in Killeen, Tex., and fatally wounded 23 people before killing himself. It was the worst mass shooting in U.S. history.

And last week, rumors of an [impen]ding mass murder spread [...] college campuses [...]ting offi[...]

University of Iowa P[resident] Hunter Rawlings, whose of[fice is in] Jessup Hall, was on his way [out] for the Iowa-Ohio State [football] game when the shootings oc[curred,] Rhodes said he was retur[ning to] Iowa City.

Rhodes said that the sch[ool was] bringing in a team of psych[ologists] to assist administrators a[nd em]ployees who had witness[ed the] shootings.

Late Friday evening, ma[ny stu]dents gathered at bars c[lose to] campus. Conversation s[topped] when television stations bro[ke into] regular programming with [up]dates on the shootings.

The loss of Ajax cast down the Greeks. Their two greatest warriors were now dead. Then, as if taking Achilles' place, his son Neoptolemus arrived from Greece. He'd been born to one of the princesses among whom Achilles had been hidden by his mother. Like his father, Neoptolemus was full-grown at an early age. King Philoctetes, the master archer, joined the camp as well.

At once Philoctetes challenged Paris to a duel. Paris accepted, put an arrow to his bowstring, and got off the first shot. It flew wide of its mark. Then Philoctetes loosed a trio of arrows, piercing Paris in the hand, eye, and ankle. Paris dragged himself back to Troy and died in Helen's arms.

The Greeks found only scant cheer in this. Helen remained behind Troy's walls, and was soon married, against her will, to one of Paris' brothers. Priam's city remained untaken. Would the war never end? Then Odysseus saw that deceit might accomplish what spears had not. His ruse held great risk but was the Greeks' only hope. Agamemnon, desperate, approved it.

Odysseus met with the carpenter Epeius. Gradually, an enormous horse, wooden and hollow, rose above the Greek camp. On one flank was carved an inscription dedicating the image to Athena and asking in return for a safe voyage home. On the other flank was a hidden trap door. When the horse was finally finished, Odysseus and twenty others climbed up a rope ladder and through the door. Epeius locked it from within. The men listened raptly. There came the sound of the camp burning, as Odysseus had planned. Then they made out the shouts of their comrades launching the fleet and sailing off. Only a soldier named Sinon remained, hiding nearby, as Odysseus ordered.

It was black within the horse's belly. The men dared not speak. Slowly, night passed. At last, two shafts of sunlight entered through the air holes built into the horse's ears. Then a voice was heard. Another answered, both in the Trojan tongue. Rigid with attention, the Greeks waited. Silently, they prayed to the gods.

DECOYS
THE ART OF DISGUISE

In an age of ultra high-tech warfare, trickery similar to that used during the Trojan War 3,000 years ago still plays a part in the Persian Gulf War. Decoys—replicas of real equipment or weapons—from the sophisticated to the simplistic are employed. According to U.S. officials, Iraq has successfully deceived allied aircraft on bombing runs. The allied forces, according to at least one U.S. firm, also have a stock of decoys.

IRAQI TRICKS

Among the decoys and disguises believed in use by Saddam Hussein's forces:

■ Wooden tanks covered in tinfoil, to confuse radar to thinking a tank has been hit.

■ Buckets of oil ignited on tank dummies—or even on serviceable tanks—to imply the whole unit is on fire.

■ Phony missile launchers and anti-aircraft positions of cardboard, plywood and aluminum.

■ Desert-style camouflage used to hide planes and strategic sites.

■ Full scale copies of tanks and of metal and fiberglass. Some possess ... which would be picked up by radar. With a crude heat source, they would ... seeking missiles.

■ ... with drums of oil to simulate ...

■ factories or chemical arms plants, the contours of some ... to look suspicious.

■ that are really intact, made by on serviceable airfields to ... Conversely, destroyed ... over to look intact to ...

■ artillery, some of which ...

■ innocent structures

THE GULF WAR

Workers transport inflatable replica of a Soviet-made T-72 tank, built by French firm as a training device and wartime decoy. Iraqis, who use T-72 tanks, are believed to have similar tank decoys.

Agence France Presse

MAKING AMERICAN FAKES

From 200 yards away, the vehicles look remarkably real—but on closer inspection, it turns out that the tanks and trucks turned out by TVI in Maryland are actually pictures painted on canvas and stretched over a collapsible metal frame. The components of one decoy, an M-1 tank:

Two- or three-dimensional.

Entire unit fits in a duffel bag.

Weighs about 25 to 50 pounds.

Can be assembled by one person in about three minutes.

Some tank decoys are embedded with panels that heat up when hooked to a portable generator, mimicking

Decoy allied soldier carried past likeness of armored ve... the heat "signature" of a real tank. The aim is to fool a target-seeking infrared system.

A tape recorder and speakers added to the decoy can

disguise the number o... personnel.

Tank decoys cost a... $3,000 or $4,000 ... to $3 million for ... thing.

Washin...

HISTORY

... ery in warfare is nothing new. In ... d has it that the Greeks hid ... den horse, which the ... gates of the c... ple. In... army un... rmans a... viets have ma... in one case in t... exposed when it ... be believed widely

Sample of decoy military ve... stretched on a frame-produce...

☑ Fake ... enemy

■ Phony ... believing ... instead of ...

■ Some loo... practice in tra...

☑ A British firm ... tanks with them ... are mostly used

... ated Press, Reuters, Washington Post

The Trojan scouts who approached the Greek camp were dumbfounded. The smoldering huts were deserted. The fleet was gone. All that remained was the horse towering before them. The war was over! They flew back to Troy.

The great gates opened. Jubilant Trojans streamed out to see the Greeks' camp and strange offering. Many of them scented deception. "Burn it!" came the shout. "Cut it open with axes!" Priam, however, fearing to harm a gift to Athena, who'd opposed him for so long, believed that the horse should be hauled into Troy.

"The belly holds armed men!" shrieked Cassandra.

"Beware!" cried Laocoön, a priest. "It's a sham!" He flung a spear into the horse's side, nearly splitting open the wood. Just then, the Greek soldier Sinon appeared. Reciting the tale Odysseus had devised to get the horse brought into Troy, he explained that the horse had been built so tall to keep the Trojans from drawing it through their gates. If it were brought in, Sinon said, Calchas had warned that the Trojans would one day lay waste to Greece. Odysseus smiled to hear the crowd clamoring to drag the horse into Troy.

"Lies!" roared Laocoön. Then, of a sudden, two giant sea serpents left the waves and glided across the sand straight toward him. Coiling about him while the throng watched in awe, they crushed him to death and killed as well his two sons who'd come to his aid. Here was an undeniable sign that Athena's offering must be respected. On rollers, the horse was pulled to Troy's gates, where the lintel had to be removed to allow it to pass into the city. The crowd trailed it to Athena's temple and there laid armloads of flowers about it.

That night, while all Troy feasted and danced, the Greeks in the horse trembled with terror, still dreading they might be discovered. Odysseus had to strangle one man and hold his sword at Epeius' ribs to keep the frantic carpenter quiet. Slowly, the sounds of celebrating faded. After a long silence, there came footsteps.

"It's Sinon," a voice called softly. "Come down."

rules, the bag should …
cted at Frankfurt or opened
ected, a procedure that
ncovered the tape re-
… eral ounces of
… been …

A Pa… pokesman in London
said th… would have no comment … had reviewed the…
repo… man for said i…
… men… said …

al treaty …
omeies …
does …

Warning Before Lockerbie Crash

cials Describe Warning Before Lockerbie Crash

… the plane. But the
… nd leg of a Frankfur…
… ute, carried no A…
cow.
… M. D'A… (R-
… mber, ex-
N.F… the Moscow
press… duce… news stories.
notice… was … ted Dec. 14
Th… places … cluding the
at a n… press office … com-
embass… ce frequented … Amer-
merc… smen, the U. Infor-
ica… ion … re where studen … con-
gregate, a… the Anglo-Am… can
school, a… bulletin board at … e
entrance … e cafeteria in the ne…
U.S. Emba… y complex …

… ni … terrorist group—using a
… innish woman as a dupe—would
plant a bomb on a Pan Am flight
from Frankfurt to the United
States.
Officials say repeated investiga-
tions after the explosion … blished
that the call was … hoax … though
it turned out to be … markably
prescient one.
An unclassified cable summarizing the "Helsinki warning" originated with the Federal Aviation
Administration (FAA) and was sent
by the State Department to all Em-
… ro … posts on Dec…

ing that some 65 "alert man…
ment service employees i…
providing all required security…
also from New York by askin…
for "specific details on lost
nue."
The commission has until …
… submit a report to Pr…
Bush … how to combat a
terrorism. First witness …
day, Rep. Dan … Fascell …
said there are still glaring …
cies in security, such
… osting of passenger man…
and H…

hristmas, Smith said. "Here, it
eems to me we have a moral ob-
gation to let people know."
The embassy's regional security
officer, Mark A. … anna, added that
the notice was distributed not only
to U.S. diplomats, business executives
ican journalists, business executives
and students in Moscow as well to
Soviet authorities.
Their testimony marked the first
time the full story of the Moscow
posting, long a sore point in the
controversy over Flight 103, has
been made public.
Relatives of some the Americ…
victims of the Dec. 21, 1988 …
sion have asked why the …
had so many empty seats …
warnings …

Anonymous Tip Warned of Pan Am Bomb

nonymous Tip Warned of Pan Am Bomb

tip: Some considered it a coinci-
dence unrelated to the crash of Pan
American Flight 103 while others
found it so eerily close to … A14, Col. 1
theory of the cause of the …
they did not disc… … if …

By Don Oberdorfer
Washington Post Staff Writer

An anonymous telephone tip to
the U.S. Embassy in Helsinki Dec. 5
… ing of a terrorist bomb plot
… Pan American airlines
… ankfurt to the United
… a widespread
… officials,
… abroad,
… states …
… lert to airpor…
airlines and U.S. em…
the State Department said
day.
But the public was not notified, in
part because tips and threats of terrorism against Americans are com-
monplace. There has been nearly
one a day since Labor Day, State
Department officials said.
The Helsinki telephone threat,
which U.S. security officials took
seriously, was discounted as a crank
call by Finnish Police, according to
… ankfurt found no nt officials. The
change security procedures f Foreign Affairs

Officials …
spoke with …
cent, said …
Abdullah in …
an explosi …
Garadat, …
Finland. Ga…
unidentified …
sinki, and sh…
vice to Frankfu…
bound Pan Am…
within two wee…
The officials …
tipster, whose …
have originated i…
the two plotters …
Nidal organizatio…
Palestinian terroris…
to the Palesti …

Lax Security Blamed In Pan Am Bombing
Key Bag Went Uninspected, Report

By Glenn Frankel
Washington Post Foreign Service

LONDON, March 22—An official
inquest concluded today that the
December 1988 terrorist bombing
of a Pan American World Airways
… that killed 270 people
… prevented if the
… ighter baggage
… London and

ing 259 passen…
11 residents …
Mowat's report …
procedure a "defe…
a substantial risk…
panied bag cont…
device would be …
Lee … nd
yer w… r …
victims, we…
ing "it fits …
and predic…
… ral laws …

Consultant Says He Warned Pan Am

Consultant Says He Warned Pan Am

By Glenn Frankel
Washington Post Foreign Service

JERUSALEM, Dec. 29—An Is-
raeli security consultant charged
today that Pan American airlines
ignored his … warnings two
… y was

view of industry-wide airline security procedures and said he would
be willing to cooperate with such a
review."
Asked whether his findings might
pply to other airlines or to the airline industry in general. Langotsky
would not comment for publication.
The security consultant said he
had been reluctant to speak about
… client … an Am, but
… following last

The team repo…
ous security …
Am stations …
It said the …
under "a mi…
cept" that in…
appropriate …
potential terrori…
an over-reliance …
… ch a …
and …
… se …
aids, and … he …
out suspects." …
… that the c …

DECEMBER 1988–MARCH 1991

The trap door opened. Warily, the Greeks climbed down. All was still. Worn out with revelry, filled with wine, the Trojans were sleeping deep as the dead.

Odysseus quickly dispersed his men. The sleeping sentries' throats were cut. The gates were opened. A beacon was lit as a signal to Agamemnon, who'd not sailed for Greece but hidden the fleet behind the island of Tenedos. The ships landed. The army raced into Troy, and the slaughter began. Awake and asleep, young and old, the Trojans were butchered by the pitiless Greeks. It was not a battle, but a massacre.

Queen Hecuba awoke smelling smoke. "Troy burns!" she cried. Priam saw that it was true. They fled to Zeus' altar for protection. But Achilles' bloodthirsty son, Neoptolemus, found them and hacked off Priam's head. Cassandra sought asylum in Athena's temple, only to be discovered by a Greek who dared to enter and drag her away. Menelaus, determined to slay Helen, was attacked by the Trojan prince who'd married her against her wishes. While they fought on a stairway, she crept behind the Trojan and stabbed him in the back. This deed and the sight of her still overpowering beauty changed Menelaus' mind. Charmed anew, he led Helen to safety.

For three days the killing and looting continued. The streets were heaped with the dying and the dead. The Greeks slew all of Priam's sons and grandsons, then found Hector's two-year-old boy. Afraid he'd grow up to avenge his family's deaths, Odysseus cast him off Troy's wall.

The plunder and women were divided up, Odysseus taking Queen Hecuba as his slave. Agamemnon claimed Cassandra. Then building by building, the city was burned. Last, the Greeks leveled the walls that had kept them at bay for so long. When they left, the hill on which Troy had been built held nothing that rose above a man's knee.

THE MY LAI MASSACRE

IT passed without notice when it occurred in mid-March 1968, at a time when the war news was still dominated by the siege of Khe Sanh. Yet the brief action at My Lai, a hamlet in Viet Cong-infested territory 335 miles northeast of Saigon, may yet have an impact on the war. According to accounts that suddenly appeared on TV and in the world press last week, a company of 60 or 70 U.S. infantrymen had entered My Lai early one morning and destroyed its houses, its livestock and all the inhabitants that they could find in a brutal operation that took less than 20 minutes. When it was over, the Vietnamese dead totaled at least 100 men, women and children, and perhaps many more. Only 25 or so escaped, because they lay hidden under the fallen bodies of their relatives and neighbors.

So far, the tale of My Lai has only been told by a few Vietnamese survivors —all of them pro-V.C.—and half a dozen American veterans of the incident. Yet military men privately concede that stories of what happened at My Lai are essentially correct. If so, the incident ranks as the most serious atrocity yet attributed to American troops in a war that is already well known for its particular savagery.

Rather Dark and Bloody. The My Lai incident might never have come to light. The only people who reported at the time were the Viet Cong, w

Gorged with booty, the Greeks set sail, savoring the sight of Troy's smoking ruins. They had no notion that they were viewing their own future, that the suffering and death they'd dealt the Trojans would now rebound upon themselves.

That night, the wind began to shriek. Athena, furious at the violence committed in her temple during Troy's sack, let loose her rage in a tremendous storm. Scores of ships sank or were splintered on rocks. Floating bodies choked inlets and washed up in hundreds on beaches. Menelaus and Helen were blown to Egypt, where further gales sent by Athena kept them from Sparta for eight years more. Odysseus struggled to return home still longer, losing all his men along the way. When at last he reached Ithaca, he found his palace filled with his wife's lovers. Repelled, he sailed off. When he returned ten years later, his own son didn't recognize him—and taking Odysseus for a pirate, drove a stingray spear through his heart.

The curses and cunning of Nauplius, father of the wronged Palamedes, now bore their fruit. King Diomedes reached his palace to find that his wife had taken a new husband. King Idomeneus' wife had done the same, only to be murdered by the man she'd made king. Both Diomedes and Idomeneus were banished from their homelands.

Agamemnon's wife had believed Nauplius, also. Seeing her husband approach with Cassandra, she took her to be his new queen. Prophetic Cassandra refused to step into the palace, shouting out: "I smell blood!" Agamemnon ignored her, strode inside, and at once was felled by a broadsword. His vengeful wife then slew Cassandra. After ten years of fighting, both lay in their own lifeblood, Greek king and Trojan princess. Who could tell the victor from the vanquished?

The Human Cost of War

After 12 failed cease-fires, Croatians and Serbs are starving and dying—and wondering why no one stops the bloodletting

World War I; Then, II; Then . .

By George F. Kennan

PRINCETON, N.J. — Sixty-six years ago, on Nov. 11, 1918, there ended that four-year orgy of carnage known as the First World War.

When the shooting ceased, some eight and a half million young men lay dead and buried. More than 20 million more had been maimed for life. Nearly eight million were listed as missing or as having survived, counted...

War Damage Leaves Trail of Hunger, Lack, Unce[rtainty]

By Barbara Nimri Aziz
Special to The Christian Science Monitor

BAGHDAD, IRAQ

ADNAN could not resume his classes in geology when Baghdad University reopened in April.

"Living in Mosul, I couldn't reach the capital. There was no gasoline, so no buses," he says.

This young student's difficulty mirrors that of millions of other Iraqis and stems from the Gulf war's destruction of the network of services that held this modernizing nation together.

The futility of war

NOVEMBER 1984–JANUARY 1992

Credits

Jacket Credits